Also by Raymond Floyd

*From 60 Yards In: How to Master
Golf's Short Game*

The Elements *of* SCORING

A Master's Guide
to the Art of
Scoring Your Best
When You're Not
Playing Your Best

Raymond Floyd

with Jaime Diaz

Simon & Schuster

SIMON & SCHUSTER
Rockefeller Center
1230 Avenue of the Americas
New York, NY 10020

Designed by Meryl Sussman Levavi, digitext, inc.

Manufactured in the United States of America

10   9   8   7   6   5   4   3   2   1

Library of Congress Cataloging-in-Publication Data is available.

ISBN 0-684-84010-3

To my daughter Christina,
the joy of my life, and the
non-golfer in the family
who has more innate ability
than the rest of us, and
certainly more patience
and understanding.

Contents

Introduction *by Arnold Palmer*   11

Introduction *by Fred Couples*   13

1. The Scorer's Game   15

2. Knowing Your Game   27

3. The Universals: What Every Scorer Does   41

4. Off the Tee   59

5. From the Fairway   72

6. Dealing with Trouble and Difficult Conditions   87

7. Around the Green   103

8. Putting   125

9. Let Your Mind Feel the Target   140

10. Attitude   156

Introduction

b y
A r n o l d   P a l m e r

Raymond Floyd has always been a special player. When I first met him in 1963, he was a powerful twenty-year-old rookie with plenty of talent, and even more nerve. But what impressed me most was his thirst for knowledge. We played a lot of practice rounds together, and he was always picking my brain. All that fire and enthusiasm made him fun to be around. I called him "Sonny."

I wasn't surprised when Raymond won that first year, or that he went on to win twenty-one more times on the PGA Tour. More than thirty-five years after we met, Raymond and I still play a lot of practice rounds together, and I still call him "Sonny." The only difference is that for a while now, I've been the one picking his brain.

That's because no player I know has a better grasp of how to score than Raymond Floyd. He may be best known for his runaway victories in major championships, but I always think of Raymond as a player who excels at getting everything out of his game.

While neither one of our swings could be considered perfect models, Raymond's thoughts on strategy, management, visualization, and attitude comprise some of the soundest golf advice you can get.

The battle-tested wisdom in *The Elements of Scoring* was learned in what I consider the best possible way—through trial and error. As an impressionable young player, Raymond tried to play a little too much like me: hitting everything hard, taking chances from out of the trees, and going for the flag. But he gradually figured out that his own abilities were best suited to a different style. Raymond was long and strong, but he also had as good a short game as any big hitter I've ever seen. He developed a style based on power and touch and playing the percentages that produced very few mistakes. Raymond could be beaten—except perhaps at the 1976 Masters and the 1982 PGA Championship —but he almost never beat himself.

As I got to know Raymond better, I learned that his greatest weapon is his mind. He is a student of all sports, and his deep understanding of competition makes him tremendous under pressure. He's also vividly conveyed to me his gift for visualization and imagery. When I was having trouble putting, Raymond told me to imagine the ball was a small locomotive on a track that led straight to the hole. "Now, Arnold," he said, "you really have to believe it's a train. Those of us who do believe can smell the smoke." It's a lesson I've called on many times since.

You will discover a lot of valuable lessons in the pages ahead. *The Elements of Scoring* is the product of a special golfer's thirst for knowledge. Read it with the same spirit. It will do your game a world of good.

Introduction

by

Fred   Couples

When I first got out on the tour, Raymond Floyd intimidated me. It wasn't that he was mean or haughty. It was how he carried himself—with an air of total command. I remember the first round of the 1982 PGA Championship at Southern Hills, mostly because I birdied the last six holes to shoot 29 on the back nine and finish with a 67. But I also remember that Raymond shot a 63. The feeling in the locker room afterward was that the tournament was basically over. Raymond had that kind of aura, and he did go on to a wire-to-wire victory.

I came to learn that much of Raymond's presence was a product of wisdom. He imparted it as captain of our 1989 Ryder Cup team, and no one benefited more than me. On the final day at the Belfry, I lost a very tough match 1-up to Christy O'Connor. When we ended up tying the European team and not winning back the cup, I felt I had let everyone down. But Raymond came to my room after the matches and turned that ordeal into a positive by emphasizing—in exactly the right way—that it would make me a better player.

That experience brought us closer, and Raymond and I started playing a lot of golf together. In 1990, we won the Shark Shootout, and in the alternate-shot format, we fired a 57, which is one of the most incredible rounds of my life. The way Raymond blended power and touch became a model for me. I watched the way he made the easiest birdies on par 5s without ever seeming to take a risk, the types of shots he hit around the greens, and how he handled pressure. And, just as he had predicted, I became a better player.

The lessons really kicked in at the 1991 Ryder Cup at Kiawah Island. Raymond and I teamed up in three matches, winning two. In the first one, a foursomes match against Bernhard Langer and Mark James, we were 1-up going to the seventeenth hole, a very tough par 3 of 230 yards that was playing directly into a strong wind. Knowing I was nervous, Raymond looked at me and said, "Take a huge breath, take out a 2-iron, and smash it." Just the sound of the word *smash* helped release the tension and gave me confidence. Once again, he had said exactly the right thing in the right way at the right time.

Raymond even helped me when we played against each other. At the 1992 Masters, when it was basically just him and me on the final nine holes, it relaxed me to know that if I didn't win, he would. And, of course, I again called on the things I had learned from him to win my first major championship.

What I'm trying to tell you is that Raymond Floyd not only knows special things about golf, but he can convey them so you will understand. Read *The Elements of Scoring* and let him do as much for your game as he has done for mine.

Chapter 1

The Scorer's Game

Golf is a seductive game because there are so many ways to enjoy it. You can get satisfaction from walking in the outdoors, from the exercise it provides, from the camaraderie of your playing partners, from the sheer distance you can hit the ball, from the fascination of the golf swing, from the challenge of competition, all the way to the opportunity to learn self-control and build character.

All of the above are fine reasons to play. But if you want to be the best golfer you can be, the most important part of the game is measured by one thing and one thing only:

Your score.

The object of the game is to shoot the lowest score you can. Everything else is subordinate to that goal, at every level of the game. For all the spectacular shots they can hit, what pros do better than anything else is to get the ball in the hole in the fewest strokes possible. That was true of Bobby Jones, of Ben Hogan, of

Arnold Palmer, of Jack Nicklaus, and of Tiger Woods. In my experience, for all the other undeniable benefits of the game, scoring well is also the most surefire way to really enjoy golf.

That might sound obvious, but I've always been surprised by how little effort and focus most amateurs devote to understanding how to score lower. Right now, there are probably more people captivated and even obsessed by golf than ever before, yet most are consumed with swing mechanics, driving the ball farther, sports psychology, and having the latest high-tech equipment. All those are worthy subjects that can improve your game and increase your enjoyment, but I think most people miss the forest for the trees. The reason people don't shoot lower scores, to be blunt, is that most people don't know how to PLAY. Not how to swing, or how to hit the ball farther; how to play the game.

Don't take that the wrong way. It's not an easy thing to know. In fact, when all is said and done, it's the hardest. Learning to play golf—learning to score—is a lifelong process. I know that, at age fifty-six, I'm still learning.

But here is the hard truth: If somehow I was given your physical game, and we had a match, I would beat you 99 times out of 100 times because I know how to play the game better than you do.

I want this book to teach you how to get the most out of what you have. I'm going to impart everything I know about playing the game. About attitude and visualization, about how to deal with pressure and anger and fear, about preparation and strategy. About what's most important in a round of golf to make the lowest score.

There are elements of scoring, things that will make anyone a better player and will let you shoot lower scores. They are specific, they are learnable, and if you take on the challenge, they will help you improve.

First, we should define what a scorer is. Certainly, it can be someone who shoots low scores, but it doesn't have to be. In fact, in my definition, a high handicapper can be a better scorer than a low handicapper.

To me, a scorer is someone who consistently gets the most from his skill level, who often shoots scores that are better than the way he or she hits the ball, and who in that sense regularly beats the golf course. For a pro, that can be a 71 on a day when he felt uncomfortable with his swing or putting stroke. For someone with a 16 handicap, it can be an 89 on a day when his slice seemed uncontrollable. Conversely, a 67 for a pro on a day when his game was on all cylinders can be a round in which the golf course won, and an 89 can be a defeat for that 16-handicapper if it includes penalty shots from foolish risks on a day when he's hitting straight and true.

Scorers possess a blend of fundamentals, good attitude, and mental strength. They are winners. If you are a scorer, you won't always win, but you will know and play the percentages, and you won't often beat yourself. Being a scorer means playing golf cleanly, efficiently, without waste. It means a thousand other things. Knowing when to take what the golf course gives and when to back off. Knowing your limitations, not just in general but from day to day, from hole to hole, and even from shot to shot. Keeping your composure during disappointments and having fortitude. Having a positive attitude. Handling pressure. Having a sense for the crucial make-or-break shots in a round that keeps a good score going or turns around a bad one. Understanding that while we would all like to have days where we hit every shot solid and straight, it almost never happens. That the reality of playing is improvising, doing the most with what you have, shooting the best score you are capable of THAT DAY.

The subtitle of this book is "A Master's Guide to the Art of Scoring Your Best When You're Not Playing Your Best." Even at the highest level, on the PGA Tour, you learn very early that there is no perfect golf, and that no one has a perfect game. The best players in the world, despite sharing golf's basic fundamentals and shooting nearly identical scores, all have flaws. But they have also all found their own way to play. It's a way that's dictated by their particular abilities, temperaments, and peculiarities, and it's a way that best allows them to score.

Let me tell you a little about how I became a scorer. I may have a reputation as a guy who gets a lot out of what he has, but believe me, I was a long time getting there.

I started playing golf very young, under the tutelage of my father, L. B. Floyd. My dad was a golf pro who served a twenty-one-year hitch in the army, much of it as a master sergeant at Fort Bragg, North Carolina, where he ran a driving range and the enlisted men's base course. As a kid I loved all sports, but I spent a lot of days playing forty-five holes, practicing for hours at a time, experimenting with shots around the green, and getting a lot of supervision from my dad. My mom, Edith, was the local women's club champion, and my younger sister, Marlene, has played on the LPGA tour since 1976. As far as learning the game goes, I had all the advantages.

Although I didn't play a great deal of amateur golf—in part because I was busy with baseball, football, and basketball—I did play in a lot of gambling games around the Carolinas, where I honed a sharp competitive edge. At first, I would play in nassaus in which I had backers. Before too long I was backing myself, regularly playing for hundreds, and occasionally thousands, of dollars. When I won the National Jaycees in 1960 at the age of seventeen, I set my sights on making a career out of golf. The next year, I had an offer to become a pitcher in the Cleveland Indians farm system, but I turned it down because something was telling me that golf was my future. Soon after, in 1961, I turned pro.

At that stage, I was like a lot of young guys with talent: I liked to hit it far, and I liked to shoot at pins. When I was hot, I was effective; when I wasn't, I went for big numbers, with plenty of penalties. I had a lot to learn, which was evident as soon as I became a PGA tour rookie in 1963. In my first nine events, I didn't make a cent. Somehow, in my tenth at Saint Petersburg, I caught a hot streak and won, coming from behind in the final round to defeat Dave Marr by a stroke.

But I didn't win again for two years, and after that, I didn't win again for four more. I had plenty of tools; I was a long hitter, often grouped with Jack Nicklaus and George Bayer as among the longest in golf. I had a good-looking golf swing, and, if my memory serves, I made a ton of putts. I didn't run into a lot of players with more ability than I had. But on the tour, I ran into plenty who were scoring lower.

It took me a while to figure out why, and to develop a different approach to playing. Fortunately, I had enough talent to survive on the tour while I was learning my craft. I wouldn't have that luxury today, not with the numbers of highly accomplished players fighting just to get on the PGA Tour. I would have become one of the many cutting his teeth on the foreign tours or the Nike Tour. But what I eventually had to face was that I was wasting strokes, through temperament, pride, poor judgment, and limitations in my technique. I also had to face the fact that I hadn't really been dedicated enough to my profession.

As a young man, I was just happy to be on the PGA Tour making a living. Because that seemed like enough, I let the good times roll. I remember being asked by a journalist what color my eyes were, and answering, "Mostly red." After a few years of underachieving, I got a dose of seriousness in 1968, when I finally set some goals. The next year would be the first I was eligible for the Ryder Cup, and I really wanted to make the team. I also wanted to earn $100,000 in a single season. And having seen Jack Nicklaus win several Grand Slam events since I had become a pro, I also decided I wanted to win a major championship.

In 1969, I played the best golf I had ever played, won the PGA Championship and two other tournaments, made the Ryder Cup team, and won $109,957. But I was barely twenty-seven, and I still didn't know what it took to sustain that level of play. My short-term goals fulfilled, I became aimless again. For the next three years I played some of the worst golf of my career, barely worked at it, and totally lost my enthusiasm. I was lost, and it wasn't until 1973, when I met Maria Fraietta, that I finally got on the path to becoming the best player I could be.

From the moment I met Maria, I sensed that this was a special woman who understood me, and whom I could learn from. Maria and I were married on December 8, 1973; twenty-five years later, I know I am one of those lucky people who married the right person.

What Maria taught me was responsibility—to my talent, to my family, and, ultimately, to myself. As the product of a close-knit, hard-working family in Philadelphia, she knew firsthand that real success never comes easily. When I met her, she was running a group of successful fashion and design schools. Without ever having been an athlete, she knew all about winning.

It was abhorrent to her to see a person waste his or her gift. We'd been married only a few months when the turning point came. In Jacksonville in 1974, after a bad first round, I withdrew with the intention of heading back to Miami. Maria very seriously said to me, "If you don't want to play golf, why not get into something else that would interest you? But don't waste your life." That shook me up. I suddenly realized that there was nothing else in life that I wanted to do, and that I had been going through the motions for too long. Up to that point I had won five tournaments in eleven years on the tour. In the next twelve years, I won sixteen, including three major championships. I categorize my career, in a simple way: before Maria, and after Maria.

My wife is tough, smart, and totally supportive of me and our three children. When she gets on me, I might not like it, but I listen. Maria gave me an appreciation for how lucky I was to be playing a game I loved for a living, real belief in my ability, and a consistent work ethic. I began to beat players who used to beat me, and more important, I began to consistently beat the golf course.

Although I certainly made an effort to improve my shotmaking, in the mid '70s I began to think about the game differently, about being effective rather than trying to play perfect golf. That meant I had to understand my strengths, and play away from my weaknesses. I discovered there are no perfect golfers, that even the best pros don't play flawless golf; the successful ones all play around their limitations. I learned that if I minimized the effect of my weaknesses, I could do well.

What I came to accept is that I'm not a particularly pretty golfer, not a brilliant one in any particular area except in shots around the green. I've got some pretty persistent technical flaws in my swing that I have to keep under control. I always have to fight the tendency to lay the club off at the top of the backswing, and my tempo can get quick. On days when I'm fighting my bad tendencies, I'm a pretty average ball striker.

To combat these weaknesses, I have to recognize—and then play to—my strengths. One is my natural touch and imagination. I certainly didn't have a complete short game when I came on tour, but I always enjoyed shots around the green, and I had fun watching and borrowing from real geniuses like Phil Rodgers, Doug Ford, and Bob Rosburg. I finally got it in my head that I could undo a lot of wrongs with a complete short game, and I took pride in being as good at it as possible.

My other strength was a knack for competition, a very strong desire to win. I found that if I could stay in reasonable contact with the lead for the first three days of a tournament—chiefly by playing conservatively and avoiding big numbers—I enjoyed and even thrived on the opportunity to win. What I had to learn was to have the patience and the management skills to keep myself in the game.

I also made a key discovery. While in the past I had become discouraged when my game was less than its best, I came to realize that the times when even the best players had their A game—when everything was running on all cylinders—were rare, perhaps 10 percent of the time. Conversely, there will be another 10 percent when you have no game at all and are nearly sure to miss the cut. In between is the 80 percent when things are far from perfect, but they're workable if you can manufacture something with your ability to play the game. That's when you have to be a scorer.

I can count the times in my career when I've had my A game. The most memorable example was the 1976 Masters, when I tied the then 72-hole record of 271 and won by 8. I was very close to the same kind of zone at the 1982 PGA Championship at Southern Hills, when I opened with a 63 and won by 3. I'm very proud of those victories, but the fact is, they were relatively easy. Anybody can play when they're in what we pros call "the zone." It's the victories that come from making something out of not very much that are the most satisfying.

I evolved into that final stage in the latter stages of my regular tour career, after I turned forty. I didn't have the physical ability of my youth, but I had finally gotten my swing to a place where I wasn't worried about it all the time. I had gotten the game down to its essence: no swing thoughts, no complications, just the target, the ball, and me. That's when I got to be known for my stare, which is really just a reflection of a very clear state of mind.

The culmination came in the 1986 U.S. Open. That year at Shinnecock Hills was the only real opportunity I had to win what I believe is the most demanding major championship. In most of the Opens I've played, the deep rough off the fairways and around the greens has always been a little too much for me. But by staying in command of myself during a week when I really wasn't hitting the ball exceptionally well, I kept in contact with the lead. To be honest, I probably won that championship with a first-round 75 in terrible weather on a day I had almost no feel with my full swing. For three days, I used all my skill as a scorer to stay in contention, and then on Sunday let my experience and will to win elevate my game. It remains the most satisfying victory of my career.

I had come full circle as a player—from having all the tools but few skills, to having the skill to make the most of the tools I had left.

○

This book is not about getting you to overhaul your tools, but to use them in a better way.

You probably have a lot of room for improvement. Most amateurs routinely make mistakes that professionals almost never make. For a start, consider these ten.

1. Underclubbing.
2. Swinging too hard.
3. Automatically shooting at the flag.
4. Not playing away from trouble.
5. Missing the green on the wrong side of the flag.
6. Trying for too much out of trouble.

7. Trying shots you have never practiced.
8. Panicking in the sand.
9. Misreading turf and lie conditions.
10. Consistently underreading the break on the greens.

Of course, professionals also make mistakes, although most of them have to do with state of mind rather than ignorance. Here are ten I've fallen prey to more than once:

1. Becoming impatient.
2. Playing overaggressively.
3. Thinking about swing mechanics on the course.
4. Dwelling on a shot already played.
5. Thinking about score and anticipating shots.
6. Rushing under pressure.
7. Practicing without a specific purpose.
8. Neglecting the short game.
9. Becoming overly meticulous on the greens.
10. Forgetting to have fun.

Amateurs are susceptible to these flaws as well. But to correct the ten that are most troublesome, you must devote yourself to two overriding principles, which I'll return to in depth in Chapter 3.

The first is *play comfortable*. This means many things, but mostly it means finding out and understanding what is your best possible golf, and playing for a little less. Play for what you know you can do instead of what you hope you can do. Take what the golf course gives you. Play comfortable.

I think this is the best advice I can give anyone about actually playing the game. It's the road to consistency. It's so simple, but it makes a huge difference.

The second principle is to *avoid the big mistake*, the big number. How many times have you said after a round, "I had 88 [or 78 or 98], but I had two triple bogeys," as if the disasters were aberrations, freakish; as if they didn't count. In fact, those triples are as much a part of your round as birdies. In fact, more. They probably happened because of carelessness or poor judgment as much as bad mechanics. That's what I want to show you how to avoid.

Here's another way to look at it: The easiest way to shoot lower scores is to avoid making higher ones. It sounds self-evident, but it's not.

I've got a scoop, and sometimes I think it's the sport's biggest secret: Golf is a hard game to play well. It's fun, but it's hard. It's full of disappointments and setbacks and days when nothing goes right. It will exasperate you, I don't care how good your attitude is. I think we love it because on those rare occasions when we do come close to conquering it, we know we've really done something.

Accept the failures as opportunities for growth, get excited by the successes, enjoy the journey. And don't forget that learning and improvement come more easily when the student is having fun. Looking back on my career, and observing my own sons, Raymond Jr. and Robert, that is certainly true. You're more aware, more creative, and more effective when you're having fun. Kids are such fast learners of games because they instinctively make them fun. Golf is a game. Games are supposed to be fun.

In the pages that follow, I'm going to open up some areas intended to improve your feel for how golf is played. Then it's up to you. And that's the most important part—because all players who have become scorers, in the final analysis, did the hardest work by themselves. They took everything that they knew about the game and filtered it into what worked for them. To a large extent, they trusted their instincts to let them become what their natural talents best allowed them to be. When it comes down to doing something well, it has to be an extension of yourself and who you are. You and your method have to be inseparable.

Golf is a game for a lifetime—not only because you can play it forever, but also because, if you pay attention, you never stop learning about it. This book will help you learn that the real object of the game, once the round is under way, is not to make pretty swings or hit pretty shots, but to find the wisest, most efficient way to get the ball into the hole in the fewest strokes possible.

C h a p t e r   2

Knowing Your Game

Socrates said, "Know thyself," and it's a trait of successful people, and especially successful golfers. While professionals almost always know precisely their strengths and weaknesses as golfers, it's amazing to me the misconceptions amateurs have about their games—about how far they hit it, how many fairways and greens they hit, how much they can curve it, how much they can spin it, what their tendencies are, and what they are capable of.

I'm not being disdainful. Golf is probably the easiest game to be deluded about because it tantalizes us with moments when the shots fly far and true and the putts go in and we think we have it all figured out. We tend to block out the times when it's a struggle, or we consider those moments to be aberrations. But the truth is, for all of us, they are actually closer to the norm.

Pros know this. Ben Hogan used to say he rarely hit more than three shots a round exactly as he wanted to. Walter Hagen used to start each round with a mental allotment of seven bad shots.

Let's consider some real percentages. Every year on the PGA Tour, even the very best players average missing three greens out of ten. Most miss four fairways out of fourteen. When they miss the green, they get it up and down barely six times out of ten.

You might be surprised as well to learn the tour's batting average on 6-foot putts. If you guessed that the pros made 80 percent or 70 percent, or even 60 percent of their 6-footers, you would be wrong. Based on an extensive 1989 study on the PGA Tour that was conducted for *Sports Illustrated,* pros actually make only about half of their 6-foot putts.

Still, with all these mistakes, as a whole, everyone on the PGA Tour averages a score that is under par. Two things are going on. Most of their mistakes are small ones—a pulled drive into the rough, a mishit approach that ends in the fringe—and they know how to minimize the damage.

Now contrast that game with that of a mid-handicap amateur. Not only are his good shots not as good (other than an occasional holed putt), but his mistakes are much bigger. Drives don't just miss the fairway, they might fly out of bounds. Approaches don't just miss greens, they go in the water. Sand shots aren't just hit 20 feet short of the hole, they're left in the trap or skulled over the green. Yet amateurs look at what pros do as a level they should be able to reach.

On the green, the difference is just as great. If pros make only 50 percent of their 6-footers, a 10 handicap would be doing well to hole 30 percent. Yet, missing a 6-footer leaves the average amateur feeling angry or inadequate. He's even more unrealistic about 3-footers. The tour average from 3 feet is less than 90 percent, which wouldn't even lead the NBA in free-throw percentages. An amateur would be doing very well to make five 3-footers in a row, and he probably averages about three out of five. So why do amateurs routinely rake away 3-footers as gimmes? Again, they are deluded.

My point is simple: To play your game as well as you can, you have to know what it is. This kind of reality check is one of the things pros are good at. (Though I find it very revealing that when *Sports Illustrated* was doing its putting study, the *only* pro who correctly estimated that the rate of holing 6-footers was 50 percent was perhaps the best putter who ever lived, Ben Crenshaw.)

Being a student of the game means being a student of yourself. If you don't know yourself, you will beat yourself. A self-aware golfer is a better golfer.

To take inventory of the way you play, start with some simple questions; if you can answer them honestly, you will be on the road to improvement. The process will surprise you, probably humble you, and certainly enlighten you. Golf's a humbling game, but the first step toward managing your game is to understand it.

How far, exactly, do you hit the ball?

Not on a downwind, wide-open par 4 with a baked fairway, but under normal conditions, how far do your reasonably (not perfectly) struck shots carry through the air with each club?

This is a bugaboo of mine, because I see so many amateurs, particularly higher handicappers, underclub. I realize that most of the time, when they come up short it's due to a mishit because they lack the skill to consistently hit the ball solid. But I also see a lot of solid shots come up woefully short.

In the pro-ams I play in, I've hardly ever seen an amateur hit a shot long. It's not unusual when I've played in scrambles to watch amateurs hit less club than me from the same spot, even though their best drives have been finishing 75 yards short of mine. When I ask them to tell me the last time they were over a green on their approach, they can't remember.

I guess this happens for several reasons. One, golfers who watch television are constantly hearing that tour players are hitting, say, 6-irons from 186 yards, so they think that's how far a player is supposed to hit the ball with that club. Two, a lot of amateurs don't figure how far they can fly the ball, but rather how far it goes after it stops rolling. One of their mishit 6-irons from 180 yards away may have carried only 140 yards, but after it took a big bounce off a slope and ran down a swale, it may in fact have finished close to pin high. Three, amateurs are used to hitting everything full out. They don't realize that good players usually leave quite a bit in reserve on their iron shots. Fourth, the ego factor involved in hitting the ball a long way, bolstered by ignorance, causes the amateur to think of his best shots as being his "real game" and to choose his club based on that once-in-a-lifetime shot.

The best way to find out how far you hit each club is to go on the course for a practice round, wait until you hit a solid—but not perfectly struck—shot with a particular club, and determine exactly how far it carried. You can do this by pacing to the ball mark that the ball made when it landed, or employing the new range finders that are being used by many caddies on the professional tours.

Another way to get some perspective on how far you can expect to hit the ball is to find out your clubhead speed. This is relatively easy to do these days with commonly available devices ranging from computerized swing analyzers to inexpensive plastic devices that attach to the shaft of your club.

The point of reference you can use is that the average PGA Tour pro generates about 106 mph of clubhead speed with his driver. In 1996, the average driving distance on the PGA Tour was 266 yards. Keep in mind that that total was achieved by players executing near perfect contact and an efficient clubhead path into the ball, and that the drives were generally landing on firm, hot-running fairways.

If your swing speed is 90 mph, which is respectable, you have to figure that your driving distance on a good hit will be 15 percent less, at best, which would be about 225 yards.

My swing speed is about 110 mph with a driver, and I average just under 270 yards off the tee. I hit a 7-iron 155 yards with a smooth swing. By that measure, the man at 90 mph should be hitting a 7-iron less than 130 yards. Yet I see amateurs constantly taking 7-irons from 150 yards and coming up short. It makes about as much sense as cheating at solitaire.

Your swing speed will tell you some other things. If you have a speed below 90 mph with a driver, and tend to hit the ball fairly low, you will find that there is practically no difference in the distance you can hit your 2-, 3-, and 4-irons, and even the 5-iron if your swing speed is less than 75 mph. What does this mean? Well, there is no need to carry more than a 4-iron, for one. It means you should probably carry more fairway woods, as much as a 9- or even an 11-wood. Or perhaps an extra wedge.

Having a bag full of woods is nothing to be ashamed of. On the LPGA Tour, where the swing speeds are much closer to those of average male amateurs, many of the players carry a 9-wood. Some of my fellow players chuckled when I brought a 5-wood to the 1976 Masters, but the high, soft flight it produced compared to my long iron shots made it the perfect club to hit into the firm greens on Augusta's par 5s. I played the par 5s in 14 under par, a Masters record, and won the tournament by 8 strokes.

Think back to how many times you've played a 175-yard par 3 and seen smooth-swinging players use fairway woods to put their tee shots inside players trying to muscle up on 5-irons. If you're a person whose drives are between 200 and 220 yards, fairway woods should be a major part of your arsenal.

If you have a swing speed near or more than 100 mph, you may still be underclubbing. Keep in mind that most pros hit their iron shots with about 85 percent effort. I know I do. It gives me better control of both the distance and the trajectory. If your irons are upshooting too high and you find yourself coming short in the wind, it probably means you're going at them too hard. The key is to find the swing speed that lets you easily hit the ball the same distance.

A slow swing speed also means you will spin the ball less, particularly if you're using a two-piece, hard-cover ball. That means you won't be able to stop the ball around tight pins. So if you're shooting over bunkers and such, rather than wider openings —unless the greens are soaked—you're playing against the percentages.

Hitting the ball the right distance is essential for scoring. Look at Tiger Woods at Augusta. For two years, he didn't have precise control of the distance he was hitting his irons, and never broke par. In 1997, he consistently hit the ball pin high, shot 18 under par, and won the tournament by 12 strokes. But you can't control your distances if you don't know them. Spend some time on this, and start to learn your true game.

How often do you hit the ball solidly?

People underestimate how important solid contact is. It's the chief source of distance because it produces a shot that flies reasonably straight accompanied by the kind of penetrating flight that stays stable in the wind. Solid contact is also a strong indicator that you're doing a lot of things right in your golf swing. Most important, solidity goes hand in hand with control because the player who can consistently hit the ball solid also has a very good idea of where it's going.

Shots that aren't hit solidly generally curve more, don't start on line as often, don't fly as far, and are more easily grabbed by wind. Iron shots that aren't solid don't carry as much backspin. Putts that aren't struck solidly don't roll as well or hold their line. Bottom line: Shots that aren't solid rarely behave like you want.

Solidity is a good general barometer of where you are as a player. If you hit the ball solidly on full shots three out of five times, chances are your fundamentals and hand-eye coordination are good enough to be a single-digit handicap player. If your handicap is higher, the greatest source of your improvement will be in the short game, and in your mental and management skills.

If you hit the ball solidly less than two out of five times, you won't be able to break 90 with any regularity unless you improve your swing fundamentals. If you can't break 100, concentrate during your rounds on playing away from trouble, and perhaps gearing down your swing in order to make better contact.

What is your predominant shot pattern, and the pattern of your missed shots?

Do you hit a fade or a draw? A slice or a hook? Is the flight low or high? Does the ball have a lot of spin or not much? Can you work it both ways?

There's no sense in trying to hit shots you can't pull off. When you find your predominant shot pattern, build your game around it. If you're going to be a scorer, you have to use what's most reliable for you.

All players have a predominant bad shot, whether it's a hook, a slice, a shank, thin or fat. If you don't know your tendencies, you're putting yourself at a tremendous disadvantage, especially on difficult golf courses with a lot of trouble. When you're on the course trying to make the best score possible, you have to be able to play away from trouble according to where your bad shots tend to go. If you're a slicer whose bad shot goes way right, and there's a lake that borders the fairway on the right, the percentage play is to aim to the left as much as possible to prevent a penalty and a resulting big score.

You might call this defensive golf, and you'd be right. But the golfer without great control or skills who's trying to shoot his lowest simply has to avoid hazards to stay away from the big number that's out there waiting for him. You may be trying to get rid of your slice, so you hate to play for it, but the practice range is the place to address that problem; when you're on the course, accept your problem and plan around it. There is no use in stubbornly trying to hit "correct" shots if you can't pull them off with any degree of reliability. If you're serious about scoring, you have to go with what works.

Believe me, pros play by this dictum. We all have a "safety," inelegant shots we hit when a hole is particularly penal, or when we're feeling low on confidence or unusually nervous, just to get the ball in play. We're basically playing for a miss, but it's a miss that is sometimes more reliable than trying to produce a purer stroke.

What clubs do you hit well?

Your favorite clubs can tell you a lot about your swing and the kind of player you can become.

If you like to hit woods, chances are you have a sweeping action through the ball. Players with a slow swing speed tend to prefer woods because the low center of gravity in the head helps them get the ball up in the air. Also, because players with slow swing speeds are short hitters, they frequently have to hit fairway woods.

If you like to hit irons but not woods, your forward swing is probably more steeply downward. You are likely a low ball hitter who "traps" the ball at impact. Your swing speed is probably high enough that you have no problem getting the ball into the air, even with the long irons. But a steep downswing creates a problem with the woods, particularly the driver, because the angle of descent makes it more difficult for the club to meet the ball squarely in the back.

The very best players hit both woods and irons well, but even the elite have swings better suited to one or the other. Greg Norman is one of the greatest drivers of the ball who ever lived, but for most of his career his very fast, sweeping action through the ball made it difficult for him to control the flight and distance of his irons. (Greg in recent years has turned himself into a much more consistent iron player.) Seve Ballesteros is just the opposite, a steep swinger who's more comfortable with his irons than with his driver, which he's often had trouble hitting straight.

Mechanically, sweep is better than steep. A sweeping swing is more sound, and from a good lie, it won't cause the problems the steeper swing runs into with woods; you should be able to hit every club well. You might, however, have trouble with poor lies, and at those times when you want to hit the ball low. (To get a steeper path on your downswing for those shots, simply move the ball back in your stance.) In the short game, a sweeper will probably excel at lobs and pitches.

If your downswing is naturally steeper, you'll be good from tough lies and rough. Your ball flight will be low, which will make it hard to get distance on lush courses, and you'll have trouble stopping the ball on hard greens. (To get a more sweeping action, move the ball up opposite your left heel.) In the short game, you'll probably prefer punched pitch-and-run shots.

The larger point is to pay attention to what you do well, because the chances are good that even as you improve, your favorite shots will remain very much the same. When you know your strengths, play to them. And while you should work on your weaknesses, as long as they remain weaknesses, don't try to push them to unrealistic levels on the golf course.

(Your favorite clubs may also tell you which are best fit to you. If, for example, you love your 6-iron but hate your 8-iron, I'd be willing to bet the two clubs aren't built to matching specifications. Go to a pro, have him determine the proper lie angle for your swing, the right grip size, shaft flex, and swingweight. The odds are very good that the club you hit best will be the closest match to what your pro recommends, while the clubs you don't hit well will be a poorer match.)

What are your skills around the green?

Your ability to recover from around the green will be based on your technique, the variety of shots you can hit, your ability to read lies, your judgment, your touch, and the amount you practice.

If you have a sophisticated short game, you can make up for a lot of deficiencies in the long game. Most high handicappers, however, do not. A good short game should include competence in chipping, pitching, and the basic sand shots and flop shots. Are you comfortable with all these shots? If you aren't, you have work to do on the short game before you start to become a scorer.

What's great about the short game is that with some diligence,

any player beyond a rank beginner can gain surprising competence. The short game allows for idiosyncrasies in technique because there isn't the same premium the full swing puts on the
athletic moves that produce clubhead speed.

By the way, the PGA Tour average for saving par after missing
the green in regulation is about 64 percent. You may think you
approach that number, but if you carry more than a 10 handicap,
chances are you get up and down less than 25 percent of the time.
In the short game, there is always room for, and the realistic
possibility of, improvement.

How well do you putt from 6 feet and in?

To me, this is the best measure of how good a putter you are. If
you are good inside 6 feet, it almost surely means your putting
mechanics are sound. Making putts in the 6-foot range with some
regularity means you can be a scorer because it's not that difficult
to learn to chip and pitch within a 6-foot radius, or to lag-putt that
close.

However, to be consistent on short putts requires a good eye
for reading putts, a good stroke, a good attitude, and good focus,
none of which comes easily.

I'll say this a couple of times in this book, and let me stress it
again: The most important shot in golf is the 6-foot putt. If you're
sound from 6 feet, you've widened your target for chips, pitches,
and lag-putts to a 12-foot circle, a nice, comfortable target. You
can't spend too much time practicing 6-footers.

As mentioned above, the tour average from 6 feet is 50 percent, but if you find that you make less than a third of those
putts (which I think is quite common among even single-digit
handicappers), you have a lot of work to do before you can say
you aren't wasting strokes. For a player beyond the rank of begin-

ner, missing short putts regularly will, more than any other factor, hurt your ability to score.

What is your mental approach during a round?

I've heard that the ideal state in which to play golf is "physically relaxed but mentally engaged." That doesn't mean you can't be nervous; in fact, I think nervousness is good in putting a fine edge on the senses. When a pro is nervous, he often says he's excited.

Most amateurs whom I play with in pro ams are nervous in a different way. They're afraid of embarrassing themselves, afraid of what people might think of them. When they hit a bad shot, you can see the fear take them over. Their greatest fear is that they won't be able to stop hitting bad shots.

A lot of amateurs also allow anger to take them over. They either go ballistic and lose their composure, or get sullen from depression. Their games go downhill with them.

To be a scorer, you have to look at golf as a challenge, one that is going to get the best of you much of the time. But there's no shame in having a hard time with a hard game. If you can remember that fact, it should quell your fear and soothe your anger. The best way is to remember that the process—regardless of the outcome—is fun, and you're lucky to be doing it. We'll get into this in coming chapters, but if you can keep the simple sense of fun paramount in your approach to the game, you'll be a better player. If you can't—and it's not easy without the right perspective —you're holding yourself back.

How much do you practice?

There is no fixed answer to what is the right amount of practice. In order to be a scorer, however, it must be enough that you don't lose your basic hold on the fundamentals. Players who put in their time on the fundamentals at a young age don't have to do much to keep a reasonable game. Those who haven't will have to practice a lot until they gain a good foundation.

Beyond solidifying and polishing the fundamentals, there's another level of practice that can take you to the next level as a scorer. You should practice in a way that simulates how you actually play on the golf course. The more that your pre-shot thinking and planning and clear mind during the swing can be ingrained on the practice range, the more consistent a player you'll be on the course, particularly under pressure.

How good do you want to be?

This is the $64,000 question. Everything you read in this book will have to be filtered through the answer to that question. It's a question only you can answer, and it's of course dependent on factors like time, age, responsibility, and experience in the game.

Desire and time are the biggest determinants in improvement. How much you have of each will tell you what is realistic for you to strive for. If you don't have a lot of either, you can still be a scorer by using the principles in this book, but only at a level of play that's within your skill level.

O

If you've answered these questions honestly, you have a good idea of your shortcomings as a player and a scorer, as well as your strengths. More important, you know better where to direct your energies and where you're headed.

So, assess yourself, and assess your game. Think about how your strengths and weaknesses fit the golf course you are playing. Through self-knowledge, you'll become a better player. You'll hit the shot you know you can hit, not the one you hope you can hit, and certainly not the one you saw on television. Once you're honest with yourself, your education in the elements of scoring can begin.

Chapter 3

The Universals:
What Every Scorer Does

*I*f you're going to be a scorer, you have to do the things that scorers do. I can tell you from experience that your education in that regard will never really stop. It should start, however, with what I call the universals. These are the basics that apply to every part of the game, and that every scorer has mastered.

The universals give you a handle on the game. There aren't many of them, and they are simple in concept. Sometimes golf seems very complicated, and the universals are a kind of checklist that get me, and will get you, back on track. They cut through the confusion, and they breed a sense of confidence and control. They make it easier to be a golf thinker, and thus easier to be a scorer.

Play comfortable

I said earlier that I think this is the best advice I can give anyone about playing golf. It's the biggest factor in consistently getting the most from your game.

To me, playing "comfortable" means understanding what you're capable of, and playing at a level just inside that boundary. It's also called playing within yourself.

It means playing golf the easiest way you can. Avoiding high-risk shots in favor of safe ones. Swinging easy instead of hard. Playing shots that allow you to relax rather than to feel pressure. Taking what the golf course gives you.

On its surface, this might not seem a very appealing concept. After all, isn't it part of the fun of golf to test your ability? Why intentionally underachieve when the way to improvement lies in stretching your limits?

Well, the truth is, you won't be underachieving at all, you'll be growing as a scorer, and your scores *will* come down, which is hardly a sign of underachieving. Playing within oneself is a time-honored method of sports performance, one the greatest athletes practice regularly. Champion boxers routinely start their fights conservatively, to ease into a good rhythm, to make sure they don't make a foolish mistake until they can figure out their opponent, and to conserve energy in order to get relatively stronger as the fight goes on. Race-car drivers drive smoothly at first, both to conserve their cars and to gradually figure out the track so they're going faster at the end.

Watching Michael Jordan play, I often get the sense that he consciously plays within himself in the early stages of a game, taking what the defense gives him, but mostly getting his team-mates involved. If, in the fourth quarter, his team needs an offensive explosion from him, Jordan is ready, because he has built momentum by playing comfortable.

A comfortable player more easily gets into an easy rhythm that will repeat. I know so many of my best rounds started with a smooth drive hit just to get in the fairway, and a smooth iron just to get on the green. As I kept up this approach over the first few holes, I might have made some putts or I might not, but my confidence was growing just from the act of doing things easily, and I gradually got more comfortable trying for more. If I'd started forcing shots early, I might have made a couple of early birdies, but the chances are good I would've had a harder time keeping an effective rhythm into the round.

It's important to make the distinction between playing comfortable and being "on"—which occurs on those rare days when everything is clicking physically. Playing comfortable means accepting what you have that day—no matter how little that might be—and not forcing more. It's a mind-set more than a physical state. And it's a key to getting the most out of your game.

It's a lesson that came to me slowly, but once it came, I was in contention to win a lot more often. Bobby Jones learned the same lesson and wrote that it was a vital part of his incredible run of winning thirteen major championships within a period of seven years. "It is a fact that I never did any real amount of winning," he wrote, "until I learned to adjust my ambitions to more reasonable projects shot by shot, and to strive for a rate of performance that was consistently good and reliable, rather than placing my hopes upon the accomplishment of a series of brilliant sallies."

Playing comfortable takes discipline, because it's in our natures to push the limits of what we can do. But I think it's very instructive that of the players I've competed against, Jack Nicklaus was the greatest exponent of playing comfortable. Even though he had the ability—probably more than anyone in the field—to drive par 4s and shoot at tucked-away pins, Jack would patiently play irons off the tee, shoot at the middle of the greens, and lag his putts to tap-in range. The fact that he would usually hit every shot exactly where he was aiming while playing so conservatively made you glad he wasn't shooting at the hole, but Jack knew what he was doing. He was establishing complete control of his game, so, like Jordan, if he needed more at the end of the tournament, he could reach for it effortlessly, without forcing anything he couldn't handle. Jack was also blessed with the kind of ability that allowed him to win tournaments while playing conservatively. I see the same qualities in Ernie Els and the beginnings of them in Tiger Woods.

Playing comfortable promotes physical relaxation. It's easy to maintain nice, loose arms and light grip pressure—two of the keys, by the way, to hitting for distance. One of the best tips I've ever heard was given by Sam Snead when he advised swinging at about 85 percent effort. Sam said swinging at that pace was conducive to smoothness, which promoted good timing. He said that the slow tempo and the absence of any violent moves in the swing gave the body time to make corrections, so bad swings didn't send the ball nearly as far off line as a hard bad swing would. He also maintained that the club traveled faster in the hitting area at 85 percent effort than at 100 percent, and I believe he was right. You can prove it to yourself on one of those devices that clocks swing speed.

When you play comfortable, you also take enough club. Rather than trying to hit a 6-iron perfectly—which I would call a force—you take the smooth 5-iron. You have more control, you get up to the flag more often, and you probably hit more shots solid.

On the mental side, playing comfortable engenders a calm, confident state of mind. You know you're hitting the shot with the greatest margin for error, so there's less pressure to hit the ball perfectly.

I see so many amateurs who are always forcing shots and playing out of their comfort zone. On long par 4s that they can reach only with their two best shots, they try for too much off the tee, get in trouble, and make a big number. They would be much better off smoothing something—perhaps even a fairway wood or long iron—off the tee, doing the same with their approach, and giving themselves a chance for a one-putt par and at worst an easy bogey. The strain of trying to produce perfect shots can get you into an edgy mental state that can affect your whole round. Professionals avoid this state of mind unless they know their games can handle it.

In this regard, playing comfortable is crucial in competition. In the prime of my career, I gained a reputation as being a good front-runner; the reason, I think, is that when I had a lead, I would make a conscious effort to play comfortable. My view was that as long as I did, the field had to come and get me; I wasn't going to go back to them. That mind-set gave me a mental safety net, and very often, I found that after a few holes I would get back into a groove that made more aggressive golf comfortable. When I've had runaway victories, or led wire to wire, that's precisely what happened.

Playing comfortable takes patience. If you aren't used to it, you may feel as if you're leaving strokes on the course. But that impression is formed because the satisfaction you get from the difficult shots you pull off makes you think of that as your normal performance. The point of playing comfortable is to produce a level of play that you can sustain. You're trading in the feeling of the rare, heroic shot for the better feeling of consistently lower scores.

A comfortable approach avoids risks because they create pressure and a negative mind-set. But once a player in a comfortable mode makes a strategic choice to play a percentage shot, his mind frees his body to produce a smooth swing unencumbered by fear.

A comfortable round is filled with one positive shot after another. In that sense, having a conservative strategy makes it easier to have a confident swing.

One more thing: I believe that beginners in particular should make sure they play as comfortable as possible. That means learning golf on easy courses, in a relaxed environment, without a lot of pressure to play quickly on a crowded course. Amateurs should also make a point of playing from the right set of tees, the ones that make comfortable golf more accessible to them.

Avoid the big mistake

This is also vital to being a scorer. As much as a good player knows where his opportunities are, he knows even more where disaster lies. A scorer knows good golf is not so much about hitting a lot of good shots as much as limiting the number or effect of the bad ones. It's a game of misses, and a scorer knows where to miss it.

A scorer is an expert at sensing danger. When he gets on the tee, he weighs the potential dangers in descending order. The worst, of course, is out of bounds. The next is the kind of rough, thick vegetation or wasteland that leads to either an unplayable lie or a lost ball. Then there are water, trees, regular rough, and bunkers. He assesses how dense the trees are, how thick the rough, how deep the bunkers, how sloped the fairway.

From this information, he determines where the safe spots on the holes are—where he can afford to put himself in a little bit of trouble—like light rough—in order to stay away from big trouble like out of bounds or water. Most holes have so-called bailout areas that might dictate a longer or more difficult route to the hole, but which avoid potential disaster.

Percentages dictate when you should bail out, but there is no shame in being extra conservative when the penalty for the wrong kind of mistake will mean a triple bogey or worse. When pros bail out, it's usually with an iron off the tee or an approach to the fat side of the green. For the 10-handicapper, the bailout away from hazards might be in the rough off the tee or short of the green on the approach. If the penalty for a bad mistake is high and you don't feel confident in negotiating the trouble with an attacking shot, take the bailout and give the hazards a wide berth. If you're basically conceding a bogey, that's all right, especially if the hole is one of the toughest on the course. The key to scoring for the average golfer is to avoid double bogey or worse.

If this sounds like I'm advocating playing defensively, I am. That doesn't mean playing scared, but it does mean having a healthy respect for the fact that for nearly all golfers, the worst that can happen is much nearer to reality than the best. Golf is a game of mistakes, and the winner is almost always the player who makes the fewest bad shots—or those that do the least damage. The less physically skilled you are, the more prone to the big number you are; if you want to score your best, the more conservative you must be. Only the really skilled can play aggressively— employing power and taking big risks—with success, and even they do so at their peril. Even for a pro, I like the chances of the golfer who plays within himself and avoids the big mistake. In this sense, a good round of golf is about controlling the damage done by bad shots.

Have a safety shot

There are times in a round of golf when the game seems incredibly difficult. The fairway looks like the narrow side of a two-by-four, the green like a distant lily pad, and the hole the size of a nail head. Your confidence, for the moment, plummets. In the vernacular of the tour, the wheels are coming off.

When this happens, and it happens to professionals more often than you think, get into a survival mode. Perhaps you can rescue yourself with a quiet pep talk, but sometimes the feeling of helplessness persists. The best weapon scorers have to handle this kind of situation is what I call a "safety shot."

A safety shot is something that gets you through bad moments without much damage being done. It's usually some kind of makeshift shot that won't impress anyone. It might have an unimpressive flight and even make a tinny noise at impact. But it will go reasonably straight, be there again if you need it, and probably begin to restore a sense of control.

If you're facing a tee shot that momentarily seems impossible, go to your safety shot, or drop down to an iron if it's the only thing that allows you to feel some confidence. If you have an iron shot over water and simply can't pull the trigger, consider an alternative like laying up, or taking out more club and swinging very easily. If it's a shot around the green from a poor lie that you feel is begging to be topped or hit fat, take out a putter and roll the ball along the ground. If it's a downhill 10-footer that looks like it could run 10 feet past, lag it. What's vital is to keep the ball in play, avoid a big mistake, and stop the bleeding.

Winning ugly is an integral part of competition, and it's an important part of being a scorer. When Jack Nicklaus gets tight on a tee shot, he resorts to a swing with little hand release that tends to hit the ball in the heel of the club. He hits a shot that starts left, flies lower than usual, and has a dying curve to the right—but it allows him to keep playing without self-destructing. After the bad moment is past, Nicklaus is usually back to his old self.

I have a similar shot I rely on when I'm leaking oil, a block that I know won't go left and probably won't curve very far to the right. After I put one of these "safeties" in play, I usually tell myself that things aren't so bad, and I make a more positive swing on my next shot.

Your own version of a safety might be a shot you truly hate and want to get rid of. Maybe it's a semi-top, or a half-hit skyball that, for whatever reason, you can produce consistently with a geared-down swing. If you really never want to hit the shot again, work out the solution on the practice tee. But I would suggest that instead of throwing it away, think of it as an old rag you save for dirty jobs. Occasionally, we all need them.

The danger here, of course, is to give in to fear and insecurity too often. The result would be a round of nothing but safety shots. If you find yourself hitting more than a dozen a round, reassess your approach. Being a scorer also means understanding those times when you have to confront the challenge of a difficult shot or moment and simply do your best. There are holes, like island-green par 3s, that give you no choice. But the security of a safety shot can be an important refuge when it feels like everything's slipping away.

Be a student

When I was a young player, whenever I ran into players better than I was, I tried to learn something from them. I got dusted quite a bit in my early years on the tour, in tournaments and money matches, but I usually took something I could use away from the experience. I didn't want to lose again and I wanted to get better, so I was always on the lookout for more effective ways of playing a shot or anything that made the game easier.

I picked the brains of the best players I could—Sam Snead, Arnold Palmer, right down the line. I used to love playing with Sam because of his swing tempo. It was like watching one of those subliminal videotapes—I would start swinging more smoothly just being around him. From Bob Rosburg and Phil Rodgers, I learned all kinds of short-game shots. Phil had grown up in San Diego listening to the all-time master of the short game, Paul Runyan, and he had a vault of knowledge. If I knew a player well, I would simply say, "Show me how you did that."

You can get confused this way, but not if you know your own game. The immediate danger is to overdo your new discovery in your enthusiasm to incorporate a new idea. That's natural, but if you're aware of the tendency, you should be able to control it.

Being a student of the game goes beyond just watching other players. It's watching the way shots react on the golf course. A scorer studies the flight of his playing partners' shots to see how strong the wind is, how long the distance is playing, how firm the green is, all sorts of things. Being a careful observer is a big part of being a scorer.

Scorers know that imitation is one of the best ways to learn. In this regard, I recommend playing with better players whenever you can. It will establish in your mind a level that you can strive to reach, you'll be exposed to new things, and if you pay attention, you'll get better.

One shot at a time

When you think about it, there is really nothing you can gain by knowing what you're shooting. The fact is, in almost all of the best rounds I've ever shot, I didn't know how I stood in relation to par or what I scored until it was added up at the end. I simply played one shot at a time.

The best mind-set for scoring is total immersion in the shot you're about to hit, and after you've hit that one, total immersion in the next one. The past is relevant only in terms of what it can teach you about your next shot, and the future does not extend beyond your intentions for the shot that's before you. Your total score at that point is really irrelevant.

I know it's hard to think this way, particularly if you're the one keeping score. You may feel it's helpful to know what you're shooting, in that you can react to a poor running total by trying harder, or to a low total by being inspired. But if that's so, then you aren't treating every shot with the same full commitment.

For some golfers, knowing what you're shooting is part of the fun. If your goal, for example, is to break 80, I suppose some of the thrill of that comes with knowing you have to play, let's say, the last four holes in 2 over par for 79. But you'll have a better chance of doing that if you forget about breaking 80 and simply play each shot for all it's worth.

Out on tour, a lot of very good players don't look at the scoreboard—even when they're in contention on the final day—for fear that it will distract them from their routine of focusing on the shot at hand. Of course, most veteran tournament winners, myself included, do look at the scoreboard; we've trained ourselves to have it both ways, to know what we need to do to win and factor it into our strategy, and then to play the next shot with nothing in mind but where we want the ball to go.

That's not an easy trick, and I suspect that very few amateurs who haven't played much tournament golf are capable of it. To train yourself to truly play one shot at a time, I suggest you pass the scorecard to someone else and try not worrying about what you shot until the nineteenth hole.

Understand angles

Scorers know the most efficient route to get around a golf course. The key to keeping the ball in play and leaving the easiest possible shot is in understanding angles.

Off the tee, take into account what your shot pattern is, and what side of the fairway it's best to be on. If the trouble is on the left, or you simply want to come into the green from the right, tee up on the left side of the tee. If the situation is the opposite, tee on the right.

Generally, faders and slicers should hit from the right side of the tee, while drawers and hookers should start on the left. The idea is to give your curve the widest sweep possible to get in the fairway.

On par 3s, give yourself the angle that gives you the most landing area on the green. If you're shooting at the pin, in general you should tee the ball up on the side opposite the area of the green where it's cut. The idea is to open up the green, expanding the size of the safe landing area on the putting surface.

Angles are increasingly important the shorter and lower you hit the ball. If you are this kind of player, you can't carry trouble as well and will have to make use of openings between bunkers and hazards to roll up onto the green. Also, because your approach doesn't land as softly and carry as much spin as a player who hits it higher and farther, you need more room to stop the ball. Play your tee shots to create the angle that will give you the most green to shoot to, and try to avoid approaches that force you to carry a bunker to a tightly cut pin. Whenever possible, know where on the green the pin is cut before hitting your tee shot.

The final angles are around the green. Unless you are particularly adept at the quick-stopping lob shot, make an effort to avoid missing the green on the side closest to the pin. This is called "getting shortsided." Favor the wide side, from which the recovery is easier because you have more green to play to.

Develop a pre-shot routine

This is a vital part of every shot for a scorer. The purpose of the pre-shot routine is to trigger concentration, to mentally announce that serious business is under way. It also gives the golfer an effective way to defeat pressure and other distractions. By going through a set sequence of actions, you become immersed in the task at hand, which is the key to playing one shot at a time.

The pre-shot routine can also serve as the time to check swing keys that are helpful to your performance. In general I try to stay away from a lot of so-called swing thoughts, but a lot of players find them invaluable. When I do use them, I try to limit them to one per round. I find the pre-shot routine a more effective time for a swing thought than the swing itself.

Most pre-shot routines begin with a trigger. It might be a deep breath, tugging on your cap, hitching up your pants, or a practice swing. From that point to the moment you hit the ball, every movement and the time it takes should be as close to the same as you can make it. A pre-shot routine is a scorer's escape from all the emotions and disappointments that take place during a normal round of golf. When he has just missed a 3-foot par putt and is understandably disappointed or angry, the pre-shot routine is the mechanism for shutting off those destructive feelings. If you're a scorer, you forget what happened, get into the present, get into your pre-shot routine, and hit a shot with a mindset oblivious to what came before. All of us are human, and the effect of bad shots sometimes stays with the best of players, but it's amazing how you can make yourself resistant to negative thoughts with a good pre-shot routine. Conversely, a good routine will quell the overexcitement that can result from a great shot or score. You don't want to get too wrapped up in those emotions, either.

If for some reason your concentration is broken during your pre-shot routine, I find it more effective to start all over. A scorer will not hit a shot if he isn't ready.

I find that my pre-shot routine works best when I can play briskly. This doesn't mean that the pace of play has to be fast; I've learned through years of slow play in pro golf how to slow down my movements between shots, and then to play quickly and decisively when it's my turn to hit.

For the amateur, this doesn't mean rushing. It simply means moving at a steady pace and always being ready to hit the ball when it's your turn. Brisk play lends an orderliness and purpose to your playing and keeps you mentally sharp.

As soon as you've hit your shot, you should be thinking of the next one. On your way to your ball, even if you're talking to a playing partner, don't let your mind completely let go of what's ahead.

I'm not a big advocate of studying a shot for a long time. First, I think it messes up your ability to visualize. Second, it creates indecision. Third, you lose your rhythm. Your first look—whether it's a tee shot, an approach, or a putt—is very often your best. If you know the yardage, and you're attuned to weather conditions, what you first see is the clearest input your brain will have. Questioning a shot is like looking at a word for too long; it begins to look strange. And beyond a certain point, the longer you look at a shot, the better the chance that the places you don't want to hit the ball will become more prominent in your vision.

A brisk pace also creates a nice choreography with your playing partners. When someone doesn't know how to move on the golf course, or dawdles, it throws off the rhythm of the whole group. Don't be that player.

THE ELEMENTS OF SCORING

Play to your strengths

If you're a scorer, you can find a way to play a course that will enable you to emphasize your strengths. Just because a hole seems to dictate a particular kind of shot doesn't mean you have to hit it. It's most effective to make the best of what your most consistent shot is, rather than try the so-called correct shot if you're inconsistent with it.

Believe it or not, this is a philosophy that even the pros now follow. When I first came out on the tour, the vogue was to paint pretty pictures, particularly with your irons. If the pin was in the right front of the green, you came in with a high fade. If it was in the back left, a low draw. Part of it was the influence of Ben Hogan, who had won major championships with such tremendous command of all the shots, and who always tried to hit the "correct" shot. Another reason was the golf ball of the 1960s, which curved more than today's ball, and performed better when it was "worked" into the target. Another reason was the agronomy; fairways and greens were often ragged, which meant you were constantly hitting approaches out of bad lies to greens that were hard to hold. It led to a lot of shot shaping.

The point is, very few pros nowadays try to hit the so-called perfect shot. They go with their strengths. Today, carpet-like turf conditions and a golf ball that doesn't curve very much allow players to groove more of a "one shot fits all" game. But beyond that, today's players have found that the percentages are with them when they hit the shot they know best, even if they can't get it close to the pin, rather than attempting the "right" shot if they don't have full confidence in it. Bruce Lietzke, with his all-purpose high fade, is the perfect example. Harvey Penick taught his students that with a basic shot, "you won't need a fancy one." In other words, it's great to be an artist, but unless you have Ben Hogan's talent and work ethic, trying to be one won't help your score.

This is obviously even more important for the average player. If your shot is a high fade or even a slice, stick with it. What's important is that you accept the limitations of this shot. If the hole is a dogleg left, you'll be forced to play to the wide side; if the pin is in the back left, you can't shoot at it.

If you want a broader repertoire, develop it on the practice range; on the course, go with your strengths.

Target, target, target

A scorer is obsessed with his target on every shot. From the moment he begins evaluating all the factors that will affect the flight and roll of the ball and the distance he has to hit it, the target is the center of the universe. If he is truly concentrating, for those moments until he hits the shot, the target is the most important thing in his life.

When I'm playing my best, I immerse myself in my target. I try to let all my senses take in as much about the target as I can, and as I go through my pre-shot routine, I narrow down to where and on what path I want to hit the ball. In my own case, once I get over the ball, I have a kind of rocking action with my feet that helps me filter that feel for the target through my body to my hands. When I feel at one with the target, that's when I pull the trigger.

All of us have this ability, but not many amateurs have tapped in to it. The key is to really absorb your target, as if nothing else in the world exists, and then let your body react instinctively. When you're first learning this skill, you may freeze up in your effort to stare down the target, but you can overcome this by staying physically relaxed. I'll talk more about this phenomenon, which is a vital part of every shot, in Chapter 9.

Have a game plan

A game plan is valuable because it imposes structure and discipline on your round. Golf is full of ups and downs, but when you have a predetermined design for negotiating a particular course, following it can help you keep your composure and stay away from mistakes. It's natural after a poor hole to want to get the lost strokes back on the next one, but a game plan will keep you on a track designed for percentage golf.

Just the act of creating a game plan will make you more of a scorer. It will get you evaluating your abilities against the challenges of the golf course. By analyzing holes to determine the best route for you, you'll be going through the same process that pros consider critical to success on every course they play.

The nature of the game plan will depend on the golf course. If it's one with small greens, an overriding strategy might be to shoot at the middle of the green no matter where the pin is. If it's a long course with wider than average fairways, going for a little more distance off the tee would be appropriate. If the course has greens that slope severely from back to front, keeping the ball below the hole is crucial.

Particularly difficult holes are also best played with a predetermined game plan. Again, this helps control the natural urge to hit a heroic shot. The important thing, whatever your game plan, is to stick with it throughout the round. With an intelligent game plan, it's easier to play comfortable.

○

Those are the universals. When I've fully lived up to all ten in one tournament, I've invariably done well. Again, I'm not talking about the quality of my ball-striking, but the quality of my thinking and my *playing*.

Try to keep the universals in your head as you play and, especially, see how well you adhered to them after your round. In the big picture, how well you followed the universals will give you a better measure of how you played than your score. And if you follow the universals faithfully, you will become a scorer.

Chapter 4

Off the Tee

*B*eing a scorer starts with being a good driver. A good driver isn't necessarily a long hitter, although length, used intelligently, is a wonderful advantage. A good driver isn't necessarily consistently straight, although accuracy is an even bigger advantage. A good driver evaluates what confronts him, knows his capabilities, and makes a conscious effort to avoid big trouble and get the ball in play.

At the professional level, it's true that players seem to hit their drivers so solidly, so long, and so straight that the act appears automatic. But even the best drivers miss one fairway out of five, and believe me, when pros are off their rhythm or under pressure, they often resort to any old shot that will get them on the short grass.

So the amateur shouldn't feel ashamed if he isn't launching penetrating draws up the heart of every fairway. If your handicap is in the double digits, a big slice that you can control is serviceable. It's true that if you have ambitions to become dramatically better, you'll have to find a better-quality shot—but if your goal is to get the most out of the tools you have, any kind of shot you can get in the fairway with regularity is a fine starting point.

Other than being a good putter inside 6 feet, the most valuable asset you can have in golf is to be a straight hitter. Placing the ball off the tee into a position from where the next shot can be hit unencumbered is THE most fundamental factor in consistent play. Most golfers would do well to think of their tee shots as analogous to the serve in tennis: Get the ball in play, or lose the point. And you don't get a mulligan if you mess up the first one.

Playing from the fairway—or from short rough—starts a very desirable chain reaction. First, the biggest disaster shots in the game are usually tee shots. Once you're on or near the fairway, you're far less likely to make a big mistake on the hole. In match play, being straight puts continuous pressure on your opponent and makes you a hard player to beat. In sum, being in play off the tee simply makes the game easier.

What about distance? Again, it's an undeniable advantage, but in relation to your ability to hit it straight, I would say that, all other things being equal, a player who is in the fairway 80 percent of the time will beat a player who is 30 yards longer but hits the fairway only 40 percent of the time. To put it another way, if trying for an extra 10 yards off the tee is going to cause you to miss several more fairways, don't do it. A long, straight drive is a great way to start a hole, and wonderful for the ego, but if straining to produce such a shot all the time makes you wild, it's simply not worth it. A long, straight one—compared to a shorter straight one —doesn't help you nearly as much as a really crooked one hurts you.

I learned this the hard way. When I was a young man, I was one of the longest hitters on the tour, but also one of the wildest.

THE ELEMENTS OF SCORING

My idol was Arnold Palmer, and in my early years I played a lot of practice rounds with him. I admired his forcing style of play and tried to emulate him. Like Arnold, I strove to hit the ball hard, to cut doglegs off the tee, to take out the driver on tight driving holes. Obviously, Arnold's style was right for him, as his record of sixty-three PGA Tour victories and seven major championships attests. Besides his extroverted, aggressive personality, Arnold was extremely straight off the tee. That ability allowed him to really challenge a golf course, much the way that Greg Norman's combination of power and accuracy allows him to be so bold.

I was different. I've never been as straight as those two players, so while I may have thought that constantly attacking off the tee was the right way to play, in fact it wasn't right for me. The mental strain of trying to hit forcing drives would, once a round or so, cause me to hit a terrible drive that might ruin my whole round. I also learned that I have a personality that likes to play percentages. I found that I truly hate to waste strokes, and that I was doing just that by being so aggressive. I became a much better player when I played a lower-risk game off the tee. Then when I got within 130 yards, I could use my superior abilities in that range to attack with confidence. As much as I revered Arnold Palmer, I learned I had to be me.

In general, I believe in a conservative approach. Unless you're very skilled, and have a temperament that can forget mistakes, it's the best way to go. At every level.

The first rule, then, of tee shots on so-called driving holes is to get the ball in play. After that, there are several other elements a good driver must adhere to.

Carefully assess the hole

We'll talk about this more specifically in Chapter Six. The point here is that a scorer makes a thorough point-by-point analysis of a hole before ever hitting the tee shot. Can it be reached easily in regulation? Which way is the wind blowing? Where is the trouble, and on which side of the fairway is it safer to err? Where on the green is the hole cut? Is the best club a driver, or something less? Does it fit my strengths, or does it tempt my weaknesses? How have I played that day, and what was the pattern to my misses? There are many possible questions, and a scorer asks the right ones. When he acts on them, the effect is similar to an expert fly fisherman casting into different parts of the river, sometimes letting out a lot of line, sometimes just a little, but always with a purpose.

Tee the ball correctly

When hitting a driver, tee the ball so at least half the ball is above the top of the club. You want to hit the ball slightly on the upswing, and you need room for the club to clear the ground.

Conventional wisdom says to tee the ball low when you want to hit it low, especially into the wind. The problem with this is that it can promote hitting the ball with a descending blow, which imparts more backspin than a ball hit slightly on the upswing. Backspin into the wind will make the ball rise, which will defeat what you're trying to achieve.

Teeing the ball low has its place, but I do it very rarely. If I just want to get the ball in play, teeing the ball low seems to encourage me to swing easier. But teeing the ball higher makes it easier to hit. When a driver meets the ball solidly and correctly—

THE ELEMENTS OF SCORING

slightly on the upswing—the shot will have relatively little backspin and will achieve a boring flight that is ideal for carry and roll.

Make sure you find a flat spot on the tee so that you and the ball are on the same level. Finally, play from the tees that best match your ability. Most courses today have four sets of tees. If you're a high handicapper, regardless of how far you hit the ball, you should play the second shortest set of tees; it will keep you from swinging too hard, and because distance will be less important, the shorter yardage will help you develop and incorporate course-management skills.

When to go for distance

There are holes where the penalties off the tee are minimal, and the rewards for hitting a long one can be significant.

At the professional level, a good example is the fifteenth at Augusta. It's a 500-yard par 5 with a pond in front of the green. There is almost no trouble off the tee, so a mishit would simply mean laying up short of the pond, the same as if you hit a straight but short drive. It's worth it in this kind of "no lose" case to go for a long one.

Amateurs will face similar situations. When a hole is wide open with little or no trouble off the tee, and the reward for extra length is tangible (such as reaching a par 4 you wouldn't ordinarily be able to get to in two shots), then the gamble of trying for more distance is worth it. Even though you are trying for a bigger hit, you're still playing comfortable.

On the other hand, if a hole is just plain easy, with no trouble off the tee but very reachable in regulation, there is no point in taking a big swing. You might only succeed in making an easy hole hard.

Hitting downwind also gives you more room to make a big swing. A strong following wind will straighten out errant shots. But on a tight driving hole that's downwind, the margin for error closes again, because the farther the ball travels, the harder it is to keep in the fairway.

Look at the hole as an architect would

A well-designed golf hole has alternate routes that are based on the concept of risk versus reward. Generally, there is a bold route off the tee that requires more risk, but if successful has a proportionate reward and a good chance for a birdie. There is a safer route that leaves a longer and more difficult second shot, but is easier to execute.

Deciding which route is best for you depends on your skills and temperament. Sometimes a risky shot fits into your strength, but rarely if ever should a player who struggles to break 80 take the riskier route. The safe route will keep you away from the disaster shot that's been keeping your scores so high.

Even if you're a low handicapper, it's better to hit to the fat part of the fairway and away from trouble. It will probably mean fewer birdies, but it will cut down on the bogeys and worse. If you try to cut a dogleg, cut the corners that go the way you usually curve the ball.

Sometimes the architect puts features into a hole that can be taken advantage of. For example, a flat spot on an otherwise sloping fairway may lie short of where your normal drive would end up. In that case, it might be advantageous to take less club and place your shot on the flat spot as if it were a green on a par 3.

Conversely, some fairways have slopes that can act as catapults if you can land your ball on them. Trying to hit that slope may warrant an aggressive play because it could add 50 yards to your drive.

If you can think like an architect, you will also be thinking like a scorer.

Learn to hook the ball

As every golf instructor knows, nine out of ten amateurs slice the majority of their shots. If it's the only shot you can hit, you are a very limited golfer, and nowhere more than off the tee. Slicers very rarely hit the ball very far, have a hard time on dogleg lefts, and generally struggle in the wind.

For the average righthanded amateur who slices, the fastest way to become better from the tee is to learn how to curve the ball from right to left. It will improve your game in many ways: You'll be longer; you'll be able to hit a more penetrating shot in the wind; you'll be able to play more holes the way they were designed; and you'll have the skill to curve the ball out of trouble. To be a scorer, it's essential to at least know how to curve the ball both ways.

The fact that so many people are slicers would seem to indicate that learning to hook is a monumental task. Actually, it isn't. What's needed is an understanding of the principles of what makes a ball curve and a willingness to go through a period of change.

Basically, a draw occurs when the clubhead approaches the ball from inside the target line and meets the ball with a square or slightly closed face. A slicer's clubhead goes into the ball from outside the target line, and the clubface is open to the swing line at impact.

In order to hook the ball, you'll need a grip that returns the club relatively square to the swing line. That will probably mean adjusting your grip by turning your hands more to the right in a so-called stronger position. Slicers tend to stand open to the target and swing the club along the line of their shoulders, hips, and feet; you'll probably have to change your alignment so that the shoulders, hips, and feet are aimed at or slightly right of the target. From this new position, you can more easily swing back and through along an inside-to-out path that will produce right-to-left spin.

If you're a habitual slicer, these changes will feel dramatic and surely uncomfortable. But if you work on them—preferably with an instructor—you'll soon experience the new sensation of hitting the back of the ball squarely rather than swiping across it. It will take some work before you feel in control of the ball, but the ultimate results are well worth the period of transition.

As you switch to using the hook or draw on the golf course, reserve it at first for holes that don't have much trouble and give you some room. When you come to a tight hole or one with a lot of trouble, you can revert to a swing that allows you to get the ball in play. But learning golf mechanics is usually a process of taking a step backward in order to take two steps forward, so accept that you'll temporarily lose some confidence and hit some wild shots. The important thing is to challenge yourself to try your new shot, and relish the road to improvement.

You can still let the left-to-right curve be your dominant shot. But chances are, once you know how to draw the ball, it will at the very least take some curve out of your slice. If you understand the principles and work at it, the ability to "turn the ball over" will be an important part of your game.

Find the right driver

A driver can be the latest in technology and be a terrible club for you. Before you buy a club, go to a professional and find your swing speed, your launch angle, your spin rate, and whether you need an adjusted lie angle. He can then fit you properly.

Next, be aware of a few things. First, the newer drivers have shafts that are between 2 and 4 inches longer than what used to be considered standard at 43 inches. There's no question the extra length creates more clubhead speed, but it also means you're standing farther from the ball, which makes it harder to attain solid contact, and harder to keep the clubface square. Again, the tradeoff of more distance for less accuracy may not be worth it for a scorer.

Second, don't be seduced by low lofts. An 8-degree driver will not necessarily go farther than a 10-degree club if you can't get the ball up in the air with it above a launch angle of at least 30 degrees. And, the lower the loft, the harder it is to keep the ball from moving left or right, and especially right. Again, the lower the loft, the less accuracy. Experiment, and work with a professional. Proper trajectory is the key.

Some features can build distance and accuracy into a club. There is nothing more important to a club's overall performance than a shaft with the flex and kick point that matches your swing. In general, more shaft flex will allow for a higher shot and a club you will more easily be able to draw. Making the lie of the club more upright will also encourage a draw. So will getting a driver with a "closed" face angle, which would be turned slightly to the left on a right-handed club.

Swing easier into the wind

There are two good reasons for this. The first is that you don't want to create too much spin—either backspin or sidespin. A strong headwind will accentuate errors, and you want to minimize them.

There is a tendency to swing hard into the wind to make up for loss of distance. But the best kind of shot you can hit is a low one that doesn't spin much. It won't rise, and it will roll when it hits. The way to do this is with an easy swing.

An exercise program can add yards to your drives

If there is an element to power that didn't exist for most players in my day, it's fitness.

Like all of the golfers of my age group, I was told that lifting weights or even doing push-ups was something golfers should never do. We all laughed at Gary Player; it turned out Gary knew what he was talking about.

We've found out differently, of course. Back in the mid-1980s, I was one of the first golfers to go to the fitness trailer for stretching and light weight work. Since then, working out has become mandatory among the best players, from Tiger Woods and David Duval to seniors like Larry Nelson and Dave Stockton. I'm told that my victory at Doral in 1992 when I was forty-nine helped convince a lot of pros to get more fit.

Basically, the more flexibility and strength a person can develop, the longer he will hit the ball. For amateurs, flexibility is paramount because they sit in offices most of their working days. Flexibility is something the body loses quickly, but also something it can regain quickly.

As far as strength goes, the main sources of power in the golf swing are the hips and the trunk. Style your workout in this direction, and you'll undoubtedly pick up some yards. This is one reason senior-tour players are hitting the ball longer than ever.

The best thing about strength is that it lets you create the same or even more power with less effort. That can only mean you are more in control of your swing, making it easier to achieve solid contact.

Don't steer the ball

While accuracy off the tee is paramount, about the worst way to achieve it is to try to consciously steer the shot toward the target. The most accurate golf swings possess a freedom of movement that is the result of relaxed muscles and light grip pressure. Those who overcontrol the club tend to grip too tightly and produce a stiff and jerky body motion through the ball.

Good drivers swing with trust. Once your basic swing has proved that it can produce relatively straight shots, the way to give it its best chance to do so is to have faith in the centrifugal force of a freely swung clubhead.

The first drive of the day

If you get first-tee jitters, the first thing you should know is that they're nothing to be ashamed of. I still get them before every tournament round. But it's rare that they affect me adversely. In fact, I believe they help me focus, because very often, my first tee shot is one of the best I hit all day.

If you let it be, the drive off the first tee can be the hardest shot in the game. There's no getting around it, either: What you do off the first tee can have a profound effect on how you play. A good drive gets you off to a nice, comfortable start, with your confidence boosted by having overcome nervousness. A bad drive can shake you up, and if it leads to a bad score, can start a downhill slide toward a bad round.

Most amateurs on the first tee rush themselves. Because they feel anxious, especially when there are a lot of people watching, they want to get things over with. They pull out the driver, tee it up without collecting themselves, and give it a hit-it-and-hope whack. Usually the result is bad, and too often, it's awful.

Here's how I get myself ready to hit my first tee shot. First of all, I hit a few drives at the end of my pre-round practice session. While doing so, I pretend I'm hitting my first tee shot of the round —complete with the gallery and the natural adrenaline inside me. My thoughts are on being focused and making a smooth, controlled swing.

When I get to the first tee, I try to direct my thoughts to execution—not what's at stake or who is watching me. I make sure my movements and my mood are relaxed and slow.

When it's my turn to hit, I make a conscious effort to go through my normal routine. We've talked about pre-shot routine, and there is no more valuable place to make sure you adhere to it than on the first tee. Once I click in, I should be able to rid myself of all thoughts other than the shot at hand.

For the amateur, it's important not to take the easy way out on the first tee by just getting things over with. A round of golf can quickly be spoiled if you don't give your best effort right away. By giving in and getting off to a poor start, you only increase the pressure on yourself for the rest of the round.

If your nerves or lack of confidence is severe, there's no law that says you have to hit a driver off the first tee. Hit your "safety shot" if you have one, or drop down to a club you're more comfortable with, a fairway wood or even as little as a 5-iron. It won't go far, but if you hit it solid, it will get rid of the butterflies without any damage done. The key, even if you hit a bad first-tee shot, is knowing that you approached the shot carefully and gave it your best mentally. That knowledge alone is a good start to any round.

Chapter 5

From the Fairway

The fairway is where scorers have to do their best thinking. There are probably more variables involved in playing from the fairway into the green than in any other area in golf. It's the area of the game where judgment is paramount.

While the purpose of the tee shot is first and foremost to get the ball in play, the fairway shot is more about options. Pulling the right club and imagining the right shot should always be an exercise in sound reasoning.

The view of the green from the fairway gets a scorer's mind to clicking. When you see a professional on television staring down an approach shot to a par 4, or deciding whether to hit an aggressive second to a par 5, he's weighing a great many variables: the length of the shot, his lie, where and how severe the trouble is, where the hole is cut, the firmness of the turf, the wind conditions, the best shape for a shot, whether that shot is in his bag that day (and, if it isn't, what shot will do). The more he knows about the conditions and his own capabilities, the better a decision he will make. And picking the right shot and being sure of it is the hard preparation for hitting a good one.

Golf from the fairway is a thinking man's game. It comes with experience, but it mostly comes with awareness. The good news is that the average golfer's chances of developing good judgment are better than his chances of radically transforming his golf swing.

Most amateurs, however, have a long way to go in this area. More often than not, I find that they overestimate their own abilities. They're consistently short of the pin with their approaches. Usually, they choose a club that will get them only to the hole if they hit it dead flush with a hard swing, and more often than not, under these do-or-die conditions, they mishit the shot. Other times, it's their misconceptions about how far they can hit the ball that causes them to grossly underclub.

At the same time, I find that weekend players generally underestimate the effect of variations in conditions. When they are confronted with something other than a good lie, from a level stance on flat terrain on a windless day, their golfing brains don't make the proper adjustments. A scorer knows there's almost no such thing as a standard shot; in at least some minute way, every shot is different.

Above all, a scorer understands percentages and how to calculate the odds. He resists shots that court disaster in favor of those that keep him in play. At the same time, he can recognize an opportunity to be aggressive and seizes it. He knows the vital distinction between the perfect shot—which the weekend player is so often seduced by—and the perfect shot for him, which is the one he can comfortably pull off given his situation and his abilities.

A typical round will present you with more key decisions from the fairway than from any other place on the golf course. From the fairway, you can score better making good decisions and hitting the ball poorly than making bad decisions and hitting the ball well. Scorers have plenty of days when they miss a lot of shots; they almost never have a day when they make a lot of bad decisions. When you're in the fairway, look at it as the opportunity to think your way to a good score.

Make the next shot an easy one

This is a guideline for every shot in golf, but it takes clear thinking to follow it from the fairway. Obviously, the easiest next shot is always a 3-inch putt, but the risk involved usually makes trying for that reward unrealistic. From the fairway, the scorer consistently finds the balance between challenging his ability and playing comfortable. That usually means hitting to the area on or around the green while satisfying two requirements—that you can get there without too much risk and that you will be left with an uncomplicated shot to the hole.

Notice I said an area on or *around* the green. Particularly if you're a higher handicapper, shooting at the green even if you can reach it isn't always the smart play. The shot might require your very best 3-wood to a well-protected green. Or it may be a shorter shot, but to a green where a water hazard or an out of bounds looms dangerously close. Your ball might be on a difficult downhill slope that always gives you trouble. Any number of factors could make it more likely that your next shot will be hit from a more difficult place than from the putting surface.

In cases like this, the wise choice is some form of a layup, either short or toward one side of the green. Basically, you want to play to a place from where you'll have a good chance to get down in two strokes and are almost sure not to exceed three. On most holes, that means giving yourself a chance at a par but making sure you take no more than a bogey.

Every golfer has different variables to consider in such a decision. If you're a good ball striker, going for the green, albeit cautiously, is a sound choice. If the green is protected by deep bunkers, but you're confident from the sand, give it a go. If you're playing well, and have pulled off the shot before, have at it. But if the shot facing you makes you uncomfortable, either because it's stretching your abilities or because a mistake will lead to a big number, you should find the "bailout" area that most well-designed holes provide. Mentally rate the difficulties around the green. Stay away from out of bounds, water, unplayable lies, deep bunkers, and heavy rough. Shallower bunkers, lighter rough, or some ground slope might be worth flirting with.

For a low handicapper or a pro, a bailout may mean hitting his approach to the fat or safe part of the green. For the high handicapper, it might mean laying up his second shot on a par 4 a hundred yards short of the green. There are no absolutes, but the guiding principles for the decision remain playing comfortable and avoiding the big mistake.

Pin high or middle of the green is almost always good

Unless you're a pro or a crack amateur, hitting a green with a long- to medium-length approach is always a pretty good shot. To give yourself the best chance of hitting the green, a good rule is to aim at the middle of it. Another important guideline is to hit with the club that's most likely to leave you pin high.

Especially on courses with small greens, aiming your approaches at the middle of the green is a very sound game plan. It gives you the greatest margin for error, and if successful, never leaves you with too long a putt.

Hitting at the middle will also reduce the times you get "shortsided," which means missing a green on the same side as the pin is cut. The toughest recoveries from rough or bunkers around the green are the ones where the ball has to stop quickly; you have a better chance of knocking it close when you have some green to work with and can get the ball rolling. So-called sucker pins are the ones cut near trouble, drawing players into the trap of getting shortsided.

Getting the ball pin high on approaches is also a practical and achievable standard. Usually, the miss you make left or right is far less drastic than the one you make short or long. Concentrating on getting pin high will help you overcome a tendency to take too little club and come up short.

It's easier to find the middle of the green and be pin high when you swing within yourself on your irons. I can hit a 7-iron 180 yards if I want to, but I have the most control and can do the most with the ball when I hit a 7-iron about 155 yards. If I were like some amateurs, I would always try to hit it 180 yards, and if I had 170 yards, I would try to blast an 8-iron. I guarantee you that with this approach, my scores would go up.

Being pin high consistently is possible only if you know how far you can comfortably hit each of your clubs, and have a good understanding of how such conditions as different lies, slope, and wind affect those distances.

Aiming at the middle of the green and being pin high on full-shot approaches will keep you away from big numbers. If you are a lower-handicap player, it will increase your pars and decrease your bogeys and double bogeys. You may feel as if you're giving up birdie chances by not shooting at the pin as often, but I believe you'll find yourself making as many or more birdies by having a lot of 25-footers than by hitting the occasional approach stiff. (And, don't forget, sometimes you'll miss toward the pin, leaving a short birdie putt as compensation for playing smart.) For the higher handicapper, focusing on the middle of the green and being pin high will make you a much more consistent player because it will increase your margin for error.

To be pin high, you must know your distances. And you must be able to determine when a shot is playing long or short because of wind or terrain.

Sometimes, trying to be pin high can be risky. When a green is narrow from side to side in the area of the flag, particularly when there are bunkers or drop-offs on the side, it's better to aim more to a fatter part of the green. Or, on older courses with greens that pitch steeply from back to front, being pin high can leave a severely breaking putt, and being long means a slick downhiller. On approaches to these kinds of greens, being short—"keeping the course in front of you"—will make sense, because an uphill chip or putt will likely be easier to negotiate.

By and large, though, you won't go far wrong if your dominant strategy is to go for the middle of the green. The advantages of the increased margin for error more than outweigh the occasional disadvantages.

Play the ball as it lies

I'm a big believer in this. Amateurs delude themselves into thinking they're better than they are by "teeing" everything up in the fairway. Then, in a competition where they have to play the ball as it lies and hole everything out, the game becomes so much harder.

I have no problem with beginners improving every lie. When they're starting out, in fact, it's not a bad idea to put a tee under every shot. They're trying to build confidence by making some contact, and at their stage of development, the more solid they can hit it and move forward, the better. High handicappers are also better off learning to hit the ball solidly from a preferred lie before advancing on. But for anyone who can break 90, playing improved lies on anything but severely damaged or waterlogged fairways will only stunt your progress.

Improved lies allow you to scoop the ball, creating bad swing habits. Playing the ball as it lies, and particularly poor lies, will force you to come into the ball on a correct path in order to make solid contact. Your swing will be sounder, your mental makeup will be toughened, and you'll become a better player.

Understanding lies

The lie of your ball in the fairway sets the parameters of your shot. A good lie gives you the freedom to choose from many options; a bad lie restricts them. Knowing the difference between those two, and every lie in between, is vital to being a scorer.

If you need proof of that statement, take a look sometime at how long touring pros take to find a lie they like when they're playing lift, clean, and place. They know just what they're looking for, and when a blade of grass is in the wrong place or the ball settles the slightest bit, the lie is rejected.

Lies are different in different fairway grasses. On the Bermuda grasses found in the Sunbelt areas, the ball tends to sit on top of the stiff blades. The bent grasses found in colder climes have a softer stalk, causing the ball to sit down closer to the ground and making solid contact more difficult.

Regardless of the type of grass, well-conditioned courses produce more consistently good lies, and poorly conditioned ones produce more difficult lies. But there is no better way to learn to read lies than to play on poorly conditioned fairways, particularly on ground that's hard and has bare patches.

Like snowflakes, no two lies are identical. Generally, though, the cleaner contact a lie affords, the easier it is to play from. When the turf is firm and cut very low, as it is on the professional tours, the best players in the world gain maximum control. Higher-handicap players are more comfortable on fairways that are a little softer and grassier, where they can hit slightly behind the ball and not lose distance.

But when a ball is sitting down, or is on a bare spot between tufts, grass will get between the ball and the clubface at impact, reducing distance, backspin, and accuracy. The exception is when your ball is nestled in grass that's growing in the direction of your shot. This lie will tend to cause the ball to fly farther than normal, carry less backspin, be harder to curve, and roll farther after landing. Shots from such lies are sometimes called "jumpers" or "fliers." A scorer will recognize such a lie and use it to his advantage, especially on fairway shots where maximum distance is sought, and approaches can be bounced into the target.

Lies in which grass is growing away from the target reduce carry. The ball will also have less backspin, and because so much grass will interfere with impact, direction can also be affected. Balls hit from these types of lies tend to curve less than from cleaner lies.

When the ball is sitting down or between clumps of grass on uneven fairways, the clubhead must be brought down more steeply in order to make contact as clean as possible. The resulting shot flies lower, but if it's well hit, it will carry plenty of backspin.

Modern fairway woods with low centers of gravity and slender profiles neutralize the effects of bad lies to a degree, but not completely.

Even the best players get fooled by lies, but knowing these

principles of how grass affects impact will improve your ability to control the ball from tricky lies in the fairway.

Miss on the thin side

If you go out on the practice ranges on the PGA Tour, you won't always hear the rich sound of perfectly flushed irons. More than occasionally, it will be the clank of skinny contact. But pros will take that shot over a chubby one any day; a shot hit thinly will carry nearly as far as a solid one, and will still spin and sit down. A fat shot carries less and spins less.

Big divots may look impressive on television, but the pros who take them have a small margin for error. The most efficient and consistent way to hit the ball from a good lie is with a sweeping motion that takes very little divot. It's the way the legendary Harry Vardon played, and the way most of the best players today attack the ball.

For the weekend player, the advantage of a thin shot over a fat shot is more pronounced. As long as it's not an out-and-out top, a thin shot will travel farther and has a chance on an approach to run up onto the green, whereas a fat shot almost always dies short. While both misses are flawed, the swing that produces a thin shot is generally closer to being on the right path than the overly steep and unstable one that produces a fat shot. So err on the thin side.

Uphill, downhill, and sidehill

Most golf courses, unlike the practice tee, have undulations that produce at least some uneven lies in the fairway. Some of the greatest courses in the world, like Saint Andrews, Augusta National, or the Olympic Club, have almost no level lies.

A scorer, while trying to avoid severe undulations by directing his ball at flat spots on the golf course, knows he has to make adjustments in his stance and aiming patterns when he's on sloping or uneven ground. The key is in knowing the tendencies of different slopes.

From an uphill lie, the tendency is to hit the ball high and to the left. Because the impetus of the flight is up, the ball won't fly as far as from a level lie, although it might go farther with a helping wind. You will need a little more club to reach the target —a 6-iron, say, will fly like a 7—and you will have to aim slightly right.

From a downhill lie, the tendency is to hit the ball low and to the right. This is one of the hardest shots in golf, especially when hitting an approach to an elevated green. Because the weight is on the left side, the tendency is to slide ahead of the ball on the forward swing and push-slice it. Because the slope is de-lofting the club, you can normally take one less club, although still playing for a lower shot that won't generally stop quickly. Aim left and allow for a fade.

From sidehill lies, the tendency is for the ball to curve in the direction of the slope. In other words, if the ball is below your feet, it will tend to curve to the right. If it's above your feet, the tendency will be to curve left. Adjust your aim accordingly.

When playing downhill, understand that the ball will carry farther, and roll farther on the fairway, but, upon landing on the green, it will probably stop more quickly because of the steeper angle of descent. Also, when you're going downhill, you can often miss short and still let the slope take the ball to hole.

Uphill is different. The uphill approach is the one amateurs underclub on most persistently. Hit more club than you think, and aim at the top of the flag until you get used to getting the ball all the way to the hole. Upon landing on the green, the ball will generally not stop as fast because it's coming in on a more shallow angle.

A scorer will make slopes work for him. On banked fairways, they can act as a kind of guardrail for a less than straight shot, or as a kind of slingshot if the shot is shaped to ride the angle of the slope.

Curve your ball into the target

When scorers have a predominant curve to their ball flight, they use it to increase their consistency when coming into greens. Pros do this routinely, and many of the steadiest players—faders like Bruce Lietzke who *never* hook the ball—basically "eliminate" one side of the golf course. Even for most of the best players, a curve is easier to repeat than a straight shot.

I see many amateurs who are persistent slicers (and in rarer cases, hookers of the ball), continually play for a straight shot. What usually happens is that they start the ball at their target and then watch it drift to the right of the green.

A much better plan is to play for the curve. On a hole with the pin cut in the center of the green, on a shot of 150 yards, a slicer should aim at least 30 feet left of the flag. If the shot is hit solid and the normal slice takes, you're near the hole. If you happen to hit a rare straight one, you're 30 feet away. And if you mishit and overslice, you still have room on the right for the ball to catch the green. The worst-case scenario is the dreaded double cross, in which a slicer aims left and then hooks the ball, or vice versa. But if you're prone to double crosses, then you don't truly have a predominant curve. If you can play the percentages of your own tendencies, you can increase your margin for error.

Your predominant curve can also determine when to be aggressive with an approach shot. If you can aim away from the worst trouble and curve the ball back toward the green, give yourself a wide berth and be more aggressive. If you have to aim toward trouble to curve the ball toward the green, be more cautious and err toward the side away from the trouble.

Play to your favorite shots with your favorite clubs

I'm a believer in hitting shots and clubs I have the most confidence in. This doesn't mean I try to avoid hitting certain clubs (although I do avoid certain shots that aren't my strong suit), but it does mean I relish certain shots. I think all scorers play to their bread and butter.

When you are playing from the fairway, there is nothing wrong with improvising some with a favorite club. Amateurs in particular seem to love fairway woods and will often hit them at varying distances. The design of the clubs, which are built to get the ball up in the air easily, allow for this. I also believe that the more creative a player can be on the golf course (without going to extremes), the more connected he will be with his target and the better shots he'll hit.

Think about your favorite shots when you play for position on a hole. If you know a certain spot is where you can hit the punch 7-iron you favor, by all means get yourself in that spot. When laying up on a par 4 or par 5, aim to a place where you'll have a flat lie and a good angle to the green, and lay up to your strength.

A scorer also knows which clubs work best for him, and chooses the fourteen clubs he carries accordingly.

As you can tell by now, I'm a big fan of fairway woods for the average player. Equipment companies have learned that long irons are a neglible asset for most amateurs. For one thing, they're the most difficult clubs in the bag to hit solidly and carry in the air. For another, unless a player has a high swing speed, there's hardly any difference in the distance an average golfer can hit a 2-, 3- or 4-iron.

About the only downside with fairway woods is that they can upshoot when you're hitting into the wind, but the solution there is to take a lower-lofted fairway wood and simply swing easier.

The other club that most average golfers could use more of is the wedge. Most touring pros now carry three wedges, and advances in the design of these clubs have made them real specialty clubs for fairway play, delicate pitches around the green, and for sand. As we've learned how much effect the short game has on scoring, it's made more sense to carry more wedges.

Play par 5s intelligently

Ever notice how par 5s are among the lowest handicap holes on the card for amateurs, but are almost always the easiest for pros? That's because the people who rate golf courses realize that the longer the hole, the more prone a high handicapper is to making a mistake.

Don't fall into this trap. By making good decisions, you can turn par 5s into the holes where, relative to your ability, you most easily beat the golf course.

Mid- to high handicappers tend to get intimidated when they play a hole more than 500 yards in length. The distance makes them think they have to hit the ball farther, and the pressure they put on themselves can lead to some double-digit train wrecks. In fact, the extra shot allowed by the par gives you more leeway to play position rather than power golf. This isn't as true for the very short hitter, obviously, but even if 200 yards is your absolute

Sunday best, there's no reason you can't reach all but the longest par 5s comfortably in four shots and walk away with an easy bogey and a possible par.

Low handicappers who can reach some par 5s in two have a similar problem; they try to load up on the drive, or worse, try very high-risk second shots in search of the ego gratification that comes with an eagle putt. The trouble is, the second shots that fail lead to far more bogeys and doubles than you can compensate for with your eagles and birdies.

Even touring pros make very few eagles, but they are very good at making 4s on par 5s. The trick is in hitting the lowest-risk second shot that will leave you the easiest third shot. Sometimes that can mean going for the green, but it also means intentionally playing toward the wide side of the green with the idea that the worst shot you'll have next is a fairly easy pitch from grass or sand. It can also mean laying up completely to your favorite pitching distance between 60 and 100 yards.

Don't fall into the trap of thinking you have to use your longest club for your second shot. If you're not comfortable hitting a partial-wedge pitch shot—and many amateurs aren't—then you don't even want to be inside 80 yards or so for your third shot. Let's say you're 250 yards from the green after your drive; the smart play might be to leave your woods in the bag and hit a smooth, easy shot with your 150-yard club, putting you in position for that good, full, wedge shot you like to hit. Once you start thinking about par 5s in terms of the third shot you want to hit, you'll be surprised by how much easier they seem.

When Fred Couples was my partner in the 1991 Ryder Cup, he told me I helped influence him to stop trying to make hard 3s on par 5s he could reach in 2 (which is nearly all of them) and settle for more easy 4s. That strategy became a permanent part of Fred's game, and he believes it was part of his rise to becoming the top player in the game in 1992.

Walk whenever you can

I'm a big believer in walking golf courses. I'm convinced that walking along the fairway helps you get a better feel for the golf course, for conditions that day, and for the next shot.

Even if you're riding a cart, try to get out about 50 yards or so short of your ball and approach it from behind and along your intended target line. Or occasionally let your partner drive the cart and walk to your ball from the tee. Trekking to your ball on foot, as opposed to a cart path, gives you a better feel for the golf course as you follow the fairway. I'm convinced that feeling the course under your feet provides you with a better sense of your target and a higher sensitivity for distance control. Too often in cart golf, a player is forced to take several clubs well across an expanse of fairway to his ball, whereas walking allows the player to slowly assess what to do as he approaches his ball directly in line with his target.

When you walk, you also have more time to be with yourself and marshal your mental game. In cart golf, players often don't get a chance to gather themselves mentally as they hit and speed ahead. By carrying your own bag, or taking a caddy, you can literally "walk off" a poor shot and be completely ready for the next one.

C h a p t e r   6

Dealing with Trouble
and Difficult Conditions

*E*veryone hits into trouble on a golf course. But while many amateurs compound the problem by staying in trouble, a scorer knows the prime rule of dealing with trouble: If you've gotten into trouble, *get yourself out of it.* He might lose a stroke or even two to par, but he will make solid decisions that will minimize the damage, and keep his round together.

Good players hit bad shots, but they rarely hit two in a row. And it's even rarer for them to follow a bad shot with a dumb one. What they do, most often, is take their medicine and get the ball back into play. And when the situation allows for a calculated risk, they can escape with a recovery that puts them on the green.

When you're in trouble or playing in difficult conditions, the stakes are higher because disaster is that much closer. A conservative play will usually work out best when you don't have much margin for error. A scorer who gets into trouble makes doubly sure his next decision puts the odds back in his favor.

When I'm in trouble, I rarely try a shot that I can't pull off at least three out of four times, and you shouldn't either. Of course, before you can make that decision, you have to know what you *can* pull off three out of four times. Knowing your capabilities is vital when you're in trouble.

When you're playing in tough conditions, recognize them and understand that your score is probably going to go up. This will keep emotion and frustration out of your decisions when you get into difficult spots. Playing one shot at a time as well as you can without regard to overall score becomes even more vital. Tom Watson is the best I've seen in employing this attitude, and it's been key in his five victories in the bad weather and trouble-laden conditions you find at the British Open.

Attitude and judgment are crucial to dealing with trouble, but in order to do more than simply chip back into the fairway, you must have some shotmaking skills. That means having an understanding of how to curve the ball in both directions, how to hit it high, and how to hit it low. The better you get at these skills, the more options you'll have in escaping trouble and dealing with difficult conditions. And until you're comfortable with these skills, your best choice may be to just chip out.

I find it easier to manipulate the ball by making adjustments in your address position rather than by attempting to alter your swing. To curve the ball from right to left, the best way is to aim the clubface at the target, but aim both the line of your shoulders and your feet to the right of the target. Playing the ball back in your stance slightly from this alignment will produce a low hook, higher if the ball is played more toward your left foot. The setup is the opposite for a left-to-right shot, with the club aimed at the target, but with the shoulders and feet aimed to the left. Again, hitting the ball low or high is largely a matter of ball position, and the effective loft of the club you choose.

Playing unusual shots puts your imagination to work. Before you hit a shot that curves or finds its way through obstacles, you really have to see the shot in your mind's eye. We'll talk more about this in the chapter on visualization (Chapter 9). It's vital to all golf shots, but especially to those that are improvised.

Very often when you hit a trouble shot, it will be your best shot of the day. The reason is that the situation forced you to focus on where you wanted to hit the ball, not on how you wanted to hit it. You might have faced a narrow opening that you simply had to hit the ball through. We could all use this mind-set more on every shot. Playing from trouble gives us a true indication of the kind of mental resources we possess—resources most of us don't use often enough.

Wind

Wind is the hardest condition that a golfer has to deal with, and the most common. It has the biggest effect on the flight and roll of the ball, and it creates the most uncertainty. Wind dries out fairways so that the course plays faster and bouncier, and makes greens faster so that putting becomes tougher. Playing in high winds takes patience and mental toughness. The highest field scores in professional golf come when there are high winds.

It's no accident that some of the best players grew up in areas of the country where strong winds blow, like Texas and California. Wind punishes shots that aren't hit solidly or that curve off line. It tends to produce players with sound swings and the ability to manuever the ball.

Most amateurs underestimate wind. The fact is, wind affects

the average golfer's ball flight more than it does the professional's. Professionals hit the ball solidly, and launch it at an angle that penetrates the wind and holds its line. The high slices and other mishits that are common among amateurs are really at the mercy of wind, especially a strong head wind. A professional will use one more club for approximately every 10 mph of head wind; amateurs need to adjust much more.

Unfortunately, most amateurs playing in strong head winds or crosswinds tend to want to swing harder, especially off the tee. This is counterproductive because a hard hit will create more backspin, causing the ball to rise in the wind and actually lose distance. Also, a hard swing is more likely to produce an off-line shot.

There are ways for scorers of all levels to better deal with the wind. One motto is, "When it's breezy, swing easy." It's good advice for a lot of reasons. It's harder to keep your rhythm in the wind, and swinging smoothly will help. A smooth swing, combined with taking one more club than you might think you need, will also help you keep the ball lower, which is a good policy in all winds except a tailwind. An easier swing, along with a wider stance, will give you more stability and help you make solid contact—and the most important thing to achieve in heavy wind is solid contact.

In a head wind, you want the ball to have a penetrating flight. The best way to achieve this with a driver is to tee the ball at normal height; teeing the ball lower will just promote more of a descending blow, which will produce unwanted backspin. Swing smoothly and focus on solid contact. A ball with draw or hook spin will penetrate better than one with fade or slice spin. On approach shots, take more club, choke down, play the ball back in your stance, and make a swing with a quieter lower-body action. Again, a draw will penetrate the wind better than a fade. Into a head wind, even a ball hit with little spin will land softly.

With a tailwind, it's just the opposite. This is a forgiving wind, one that will take your shots out longer and straighten them out a bit as well. Off the tee, you might tee the ball a little higher and give it a healthy hit. If you have trouble getting your driver in the air, a 3-wood might be a good choice. On approaches, take less club in an effort to get the ball in the air, perhaps playing the ball a little more forward in your stance. (Be aware, however, that a tailwind doesn't help you as much as a head wind of the same strength hurts you. A two-club head wind is probably just a one-club tailwind.) The problem in a tailwind is getting approach shots to stop on the green, because the ball comes in faster, on a shallower angle, and with less backspin. I like to hit high fades downwind, because they come into the green on the steepest angle and with the most backspin. I often take the least club I can reach the green with and swing harder, trying to hit a high approach that has a better chance of stopping quickly. It's key in a tailwind to try to find the most receptive area for the ball to land; sometimes, the best way to play is to land short of the green and bounce up.

In crosswinds, accuracy and solid contact are paramount. You have to know your ball flight and play the crosswind accordingly. If you're going for distance, you can ride the wind with your curve. If your ball flight is against the wind, this will help stop the ball on the green. Pros call this a hold shot, and it can be very valuable in stopping approaches on firm greens.

No matter how well you hit the ball in wind, your accuracy will be impaired. Some good shots won't turn out so well. Adjust by aiming farther away from trouble than usual, and by taking fewer chances. Resolve to be mentally strong. Make a deal with yourself before the round that the conditions are going to be difficult and that you'll accept some bad results from well-played shots—and hold to it when you feel the frustration that wind can produce.

Rough

The second most difficult condition in golf is heavy rough. The U.S. Open builds its championship on a competitor's ability to both avoid and negotiate rough that is designed to cost a player who hits into it an average of half a stroke a hole.

Most rough on public and private courses isn't nearly as severe as the thick, four-inch variety the USGA cultivates. But rough of any type is still designed to make shots harder. The options it produces can range from having to wedge out sideways into the fairway to actually being able to hit the ball farther than you could from the short grass. It all depends on the lie, and a scorer knows how to determine what his lie in the rough will allow him to do.

In a normal lie in the rough, the ball sits lower in the grass, and will not come out cleanly. Because grass will get between the club and the ball at impact, distance will be impaired, as will spin and control. Unless the ball is near the top of the grass, or in grass that's growing in the direction of your target, most rough won't let you do anything too fancy. The key will be to get out and advance the ball down the fairway.

Very strong players can hit the ball farther out of the rough than players with slower clubhead speeds—but that doesn't give the strong player license to whale away. The problem with rough is that it doesn't allow much control of the ball. The ball comes out with little spin, is very difficult to curve or hit at a predictable height, and tends to squirt either left or right. Even if a strong player can reach the green from a heavy lie in the rough, it's unlikely the ball will stay on the putting surface. That's why a conservative philosophy from the rough is usually best.

The foremost consideration should be to get your ball back in position in the fairway. That means that you shouldn't try to hit a wood or a long iron unless the ball is sitting on top of the grass.

The key is how much grass will get between the club and the ball at impact. If it's minimal, a less lofted iron or even fairway wood can be used. But if it's a certainty that you're going to have a thick layer of grass between the club and the ball, then use a short iron or wedge and take your medicine.

Once a scorer has determined the kind of lie he has, he takes practice swings to determine the resistance of the rough. Some grasses are wispy even though they might appear dense, and allow the club to come through faster. Others, like Bermuda, have very thick and heavy blades, and are like hitting through Velcro.

If the lie is heavy, take a short iron or wedge. If the ball is sitting higher in the grass, or the grass is not especially thick, you can use more club. Be aware, though, that using an iron with less loft than a 6-iron is risky in the rough. It's hard to get the ball up, and the grass will have a tendency to wrap around the hosel, shutting the clubface and causing a pull that will probably stay in the rough and put you in worse trouble.

Unlike those long irons, however, a fairway wood is often the ideal choice for getting the cleanest hit and maximum distance from the rough. The new low-profile woods are especially effective from the rough, which is one reason they've become so popular on the professional tours. For the amateur with an average swing speed in the 85 mph range, I believe 7- and even 9-woods can be the most valuable clubs in the bag, especially from the rough, sand, or general bad lies. Older players and women who swing at 75 mph or slower can go all the way to 11- or even 13-woods—though their limitation is that it's hard to hit them low or to curve them.

If the rough is heavy, the best method for extricating yourself is to take a more upright swing that produces a steeper downswing, the purpose being to give the long grass less of a chance to grab the clubhead and shut it down. Choking down on the club and opening the face will also help, because it will help the ball get up out of the grass more quickly. A firmer grip can help here, too.

When the ball is sitting up in the rough, with the grass growing toward the target, it's a flier condition. It becomes even more of one when the grass is damp. At impact, some grass will get between the club and the ball, but it won't impede the speed of the club. As a result, the ball will shoot out full speed, but with less spin. This ball is likely to fly farther than a solid shot from a good fairway lie, and will definitely not stop as well. It's why shots the pros hit from the rough often bound over the green.

Having a flier can help you get distance, especially for a second shot on a long par 4 or 5 that you want to hit as far as you can. But on an approach, it's best to bounce the ball into the green from a flier lie.

Fairway bunkers

Fairway bunkers present one of the most difficult challenges in golf, but there's no reason they have to be the disaster that they often become for amateurs.

The simpler you make fairway bunker shots, the easier they will be. First of all, there's no magical technique necessary. The main thing to avoid at all costs is leaving the ball in the bunker. About the only way that can happen is if you hit behind the ball or don't clear the front lip.

The first mistake, assuming the lie is relatively clean, is one of execution: Unless the ball is partially buried or in a severe fried egg, you should never take sand before striking the ball. If there is ever time to err toward thin rather than fat contact, it's in a fairway bunker.

The second mistake is one of judgment: not using a club with enough loft to clear the lip. You should never let this happen, especially if you're playing short of the green. If you're laying up from the sand and have any doubt about which club to hit, always take the club with more loft to make sure you clear the tip comfortably. Even if you're going for the green, err toward the safe side in terms of clearing the lip. Failing to get out of a fairway bunker is the kind of mistake that can lead to a big number.

After entering the bunker, check your lie. If you can get the club on the ball without having to take sand, you can be relatively aggressive. If you're trying to advance the ball as far as possible on a par 5 or long par 4, you can even take a wood or a long iron, assuming you don't have to clear a high lip. Take a solid stance by twisting your feet in the sand to ensure you don't sink during your swing. Make a swing that's quiet in terms of lower-body motion, and keep your focus on the top of the golf ball. You must focus on hitting this shot cleanly and perhaps a little thin. As long as you don't skull it or hit it so thin that it hits the lip, you should be out and down the fairway.

Hitting the green from a fairway bunker requires an extra dose of skill. First of all, the target must be accessible. A green guarded by water or one that's heavily bunkered will require good contact and a ball that carries, not one that runs up. If you're a middle handicapper, the percentages are probably not with you pulling off this shot; choose a good layup spot instead. But if the green is fairly open, you can have a go—with a few adjustments. Take at least a club, and probably two clubs, more than you would for the same yardage from a good lie in the fairway. Again, make sure you don't hit behind the ball, but understand that if you hit the ball too thinly, it won't carry far enough. Unlike in the rough, you don't want a steep angle into the ball on this shot, but more of a sweep. A fairway-bunker shot is easier to execute by playing for a fade rather than a draw.

When the lie is bad in a fairway bunker, take your medicine and simply get back in play by playing more of an explosion with a short iron or wedge.

Trees

Trees present the opportunity for imaginative shotmaking more than any other problem on the golf course.

Pros can do wondrous things out of trees. But pros have tremendous tools in terms of being able to hit the ball low, high, or with a dramatic curve. Amateurs don't have the same abilities, and shouldn't try the same shots.

The lie dictates what a player can do under trees. From a clean or bare lie, it's relatively easy to manuever the ball, particularly with a low shot. But if the ball is in rough, it becomes very difficult to either hit it low, curve it, or hit it very far. Heavy lies under trees usually require some kind of chip out into the fairway.

When the ground under the trees is covered with loose leaves or pine straw, you'll have to exercise some judgment. If the ball is sitting on top, the best way to play the shot is to pick the ball in much the same way you would in a fairway bunker. (A word of caution: don't ground your club in leaves or pine straw, as the looseness could easily cause your ball to move, resulting in a penalty stroke. Similarly, lifting leaves or straw around your ball can also cause it to move.) If your ball is partially or fully covered by the dead foliage, you won't be able to hit it cleanly or very far, so it's best to take a short iron or wedge and simply try to get the ball back into the fairway.

When a tree is restricting either your backswing or follow-through, rehearse the shot until the movement becomes ingrained and you can pull it off without flinching. Again, when you're restricted in this way, a conservative path is the best.

Assuming you have a shot at going through, around, over, or under trees, there are several keys. The first is to really see the shot in terms of its flight through the opening you've chosen. Mental abilities are paramount here; you first have to visualize the shot, and then you have to feel the movements that will make it happen.

In general, a recovery shot from trees is made with an accuracy-oriented swing. Use less leg action, choke down on the club, and swing smoothly. In order to have precise alignment, it's a good idea to use an intermediate target, some mark on the ground a few feet ahead of your ball that's directly on your chosen line. Solid contact and control of the height is paramount.

If you're going under, make sure you hit a club that you know you can hit low. A solid shot won't do you any good if it hits more limbs and bounces into more trouble.

If you're going over trees, the task is different. You'll need a full swing, one that emphasizes height. That means playing the ball more forward, opening the face of the club slightly, and swinging with some speed. Ideally, you'll have a lie with some grass under the ball; trying to hit a high shot from a bare lie is risky, even for a good player.

Sometimes, a scorer has to take extreme measures in the trees in order to avoid an unplayable lie penalty. When the ball is wedged against a trunk, a left-handed shot might be enough to get the ball back to safety. When hitting this shot, turn the club on its toe, or use the backside of a putter. Make sure you make several practice swings so you can feel your left side releasing into the shot. Remember, a left-handed shot is only meant to get the ball back to the fairway; don't try it if you need to hit the ball more than 50 or so yards.

The other shot for this situation is a backhander in which you turn your back to the target, stand right next to the ball, and with your right hand only, swing the club toward the target.

Again, this is only for emergencies when a safe path for the ball exists.

Remember, trees can be places for heroics, but always think damage control first. Don't think of them as 90 percent air.

Once a year or so, go into the woods and practice these shots. You hope you'll never need them, but if you do, you'll be glad you rehearsed them.

Remember, trees can be places for heroics, but always think damage control first.

Rain

Playing in rain is mostly a matter of preparation. If you have dry towels, a good umbrella, and proper, roomy, rain gear, you can play a fairly normal round from a cart or with a caddy. The challenge is greater if you're carrying your own bag, but it can still be done if you're organized.

The biggest issue is keeping your hands dry. If you wear a glove, use a waterproof model, and alternate between two during the round. (Hang the glove you're not using from the spokes of your umbrella to keep it dry.) Keep your towels covered, and dry your hands while under an umbrella, inside a cart, or under a tree. This should keep you dry in everything but a steady deluge.

Playing in rain can actually make scoring easier for good players. When the fairways are wet, they become effectively wider because they give up less roll. And when greens are soggy, it's easier to shoot at the pin, and usually easier to putt because the greens get slower and break less.

Those advantages might be neutralized for the weekend player because a wet course will play longer; the ground will give up little roll, and the extra clothing you wear along with the cold in your hands will make it harder to make a full swing.

When playing in wet conditions, try to sweep the ball off the fairway. Hitting down abruptly will make clean contact difficult, make the dreaded fat shot more of a possibility, and cause more shots that literally squirt left or right.

If your normal tee shot is of the low, running variety, you might switch to a 3-wood off the tee for more carry when it's wet. In the sand, take less sand behind the ball and swing a little harder to move the water-soaked sand. On the greens, play for less break and stroke the ball more firmly.

Playing from a divot hole

The first step in dealing with a ball in a divot is mentally overcoming the unfairness of it. Once you accept that golf was never meant to be fair, you can go about hitting what is often not that difficult a shot.

If the divot hole is not that deep and the ball is sitting cleanly and not up against one of the edges, there's is no reason you can't hit an effective shot. The key, as always, is solid contact.

To get down into a divot without hitting the ground behind it, come into the shot from a steeper angle than normal by setting the hands ahead of the ball at address and choking down on the club slightly. Take one more club. If you can run the ball onto the green, try to punch the shot low. If you have to carry an obstacle, favor a fade.

If the ball is against an edge, or well down in a deep divot, it's a tougher shot. Make the downswing even steeper and hit the ball with a downward punching action. It will come out low, without a lot of spin, and will run. Take a club or two extra, and choke down. Again, you'd rather hit the ball thin than fat.

Hardpan

The best way to play a hardpan shot is similar to a fairway bunker: A sweeping action is best. If you come down abruptly, there's almost no margin for error. Choke down, use less leg action, relax your arms and wrists, and take at least one more club. If you make good contact, you'll probably put plenty of backspin on the ball because there's no grass to interface.

As you get more confident with the shot, you can play it back in your stance and hit down on it more, what we call on tour "trapping" the ball. But remember, a fat shot off hard turf will travel a lot less than a thin one.

Playing out of a water hazard

You won't have too many chances to do this, but there are times when it makes sense to advance the ball from a hazard rather than take a penalty stroke, particularly around the green.

In order to be hittable, a ball has to be on the edge of a hazard. Except on the shortest shots, at least part of the ball has to be above the surface. Any shot in which the ball is completely submerged is very risky, in part because refraction makes it very difficult to tell just how far underwater the ball is.

The best place to come out of the water is around the green. It's possible to pop the ball out and have it land softly, much like a sand shot. If you're around the green and the ball is completely submerged, have the club enter the water at least six inches behind the ball.

From off the fairway, if you can move the ball 10 or more yards and into a much better position than you would have if you dropped, then hitting out of the water is a worthwhile gamble.

Take a sand wedge, which has the heaviest clubhead, keep the face square so the bounce on the club is minimized, and make sure to get under the ball. If you don't, the ball will stay right where it is. Wear rain clothes and be prepared to get splattered.

Practice trouble shots

A scorer hones unusual shots on the practice range, or takes time during practice rounds to experiment with extreme measures like water shots or the backhander from trees.

Actually, practicing these shots can be fun. Devote a part of every practice session to learning how to intentionally curve the ball in either direction, or hit it high or low—the recovery shots you'll need most often. You can learn a lot about the cause and effect of the golf swing by going to extremes. Most important, you'll learn what you need when you face a recovery shot on the golf course.

Know the rules

Knowing the rules is always an advantage, but it's especially important when you've hit into trouble. In particular, you should know your options when you hit into a water hazard, into a lateral water hazard, or when you want to invoke the unplayable-lie rule.

When your ball goes into a water hazard, you basically have three options: You can play the ball in the hazard without penalty; take a one-stroke penalty and make an imaginary line between the hole and the point of entry, going back as far as you want on that line; or go back to the spot where you hit your last shot and take a one-stroke penalty.

When you hit into a lateral hazard, you can play the ball; take a penalty stroke and drop two club lengths from where the ball entered the hazard or at a point on the other side of the hazard, equidistant from the hole; or take a penalty stroke and go back to the point from where you hit your last shot.

With the unplayable-ball options, all of which carry a one-stroke penalty, you can go back to where you hit your last shot, drop within two club lengths of where the ball lies, no closer to the hole; or drop anywhere along an imaginary line back from the hole through where the ball lies. If you're in command of this rule, it can help you drop out of trouble rather than continuing to thrash at a hopeless situation.

In wet weather, be aware of the casual water rule: Any time your ball or your stance is in a visible, temporary accumulation of water, you are entitled to lift and clean your ball, and drop it onto the nearest point that avoids casual water, but is no nearer the hole.

I learned the importance of knowing the rules the hard way, but at least I learned it early. As a fifteen-year-old playing in a junior tournament in North Carolina, I was 1 up on the sixteenth tee when my opponent hit his drive onto the street that ran along the right side of the hole. The street was out of bounds, but we could see that the ball was still moving when a truck ran over it and somehow knocked the ball back onto the golf course. When an official ruled—correctly—that the ball was in play under rule 19-1, I was infuriated and sure I was being cheated. I lost the sixteenth hole and went on to lose the match. Later, I realized that, had I known the rules, I would not have lost my composure. Since that day, I've made it my business not to be surprised by the rules, and whenever possible to use them to my advantage.

Chapter 7

Around the Green

Now for my favorite part of golf, and an indispensable area for anyone who wants to be a scorer: the short game. For me, the short game comprises all the shots within 60 yards of the hole—*the* scoring area.

For the touring pro, the short game is his most important weapon for producing low scores and preventing high ones. For the high handicapper, improving the short game is the quickest and easiest way to cut strokes from his game. It's the place you can turn three shots into two. For any player, it's the key to being a scorer.

Think about this: A full 65 percent of all shots in a round by players ranging from tour level to 15 handicaps are hit within 100 yards of the green. For players who can't break 90, that figure rises to almost 80 percent. It's obvious to me that any golfer can benefit tremendously by improving his short game.

Touring pros have gotten that message, and I firmly believe

that the biggest improvement in the quality of play in professional golf today—more than improved equipment, better swings, and better fitness—has to do with the attention being paid to the short game. Improved course conditions—lusher fairways, more uniform sand—have made getting up and down a little easier, and so has the widespread use of the 60-degree wedge. But nothing has increased our short-game proficiency more than sheer urgency. Once it became accepted fact that chipping, pitching, sand play, and putting were more vital to scoring than tee-to-green play, the pros began putting more time into their short-game practice. They began to realize that while there are a lot of pretty swings and a lot of very good ball strikers, those without good short games very seldom win. Consistent winners, at every level of golf, all have good short games.

We're now entering the area of the game where execution is vital. While you can make gains in the long game by simply playing better strategically, in the shots from within 60 yards, including putting, you have to gain command of the techniques to be effective. Strategy is also involved in the short game, but if you're weak in these areas physically, you'll simply have to practice and get better, preferably under the guidance of a teaching professional.

That's the bad news. But the good news is that every single golfer has the physical skills to be good around and on the greens. These areas don't require unusual strength or timing. They simply require knowledge and practice.

What's so rewarding about developing a good short game is that it's much easier to keep it at a high level than the long game. There are fewer moving parts than in the full swing, and experience and judgment play a more significant role. I like to compare the short game to defense in the NBA: Defense is based primarily on effort and knowledge, two things that, if you're disciplined, won't fluctuate as much as the act of shooting the basketball. Consequently, teams that have strong defenses are more consistent, and more reliable under pressure. The short game is the same: Once you have a good one, you can count on it.

Possessing a short game with true command gives a golfer the most effective edge he can have, because it's the ultimate eraser of mistakes. The short game is the safety net that protects good rounds and keeps bad rounds from being terrible. In many ways, I won the U.S. Open at Shinnecock Hills with a first-round 75 in which I hit only six greens in regulation, had a double bogey, and took two unplayable lies. The average score that day was 78, and if my short game hadn't been in top form I would have shot in the 80s.

The main reason I love the short game is that it's where creativity and imagination are rewarded more than anywhere else in golf. Now that advanced technology has produced a golf ball that curves less, and golf clubs are designed specifically to hit straighter-flying shots, it may be that the short game is the last refuge of true artistry in the game.

Once you become good at the short game, it transforms you as a golfer. A good short game greatly reduces the pressure to hit your long shots well: That fact alone may actually improve your ball striking. When you're playing well and feeling confident, a good short game allows you to be aggressive because you know you can recover from a lost gamble. When you're playing poorly, a good short game makes it easier to stay patient and weather the storm. Instead of being down and discouraged after a bad approach, you look forward to the opportunity to make a great up and down. In fact, you relish it, knowing that you can pull it off, it will energize you, and it will deflate your opponent. That's the attitude of a winner. Believe me, there is no player harder to beat head-to-head than one with an outstanding short game.

There are lots of ways to hit shots around greens. Not everyone has the ability to hit majestic long shots—but nearly all of us have the capacity to have a good short game.

Which wedges?

As the importance of the short game has become clearer, the tools have become more advanced. The design of wedges has become more varied, so that there is sure to be a club or combination of clubs that best suits your game and the course you're playing.

Today, most professionals carry three wedges: a pitching wedge with between 48 and 51 degrees of loft, a sand wedge with between 54 and 57 degrees of loft, and a lob wedge with between 59 and 62 degrees of loft. The newest addition to the trio is the lob wedge. It works for professionals for several reasons. It stops the ball beautifully on greens that are very fast, firm, and have tabletop-like targets, which are the prevalent type played on tour. Its design makes it easy to hit from the fairway, and from a good lie it's a very effective sand club. And professionals can use the club from as much as 100 yards because they can generate the necessary clubhead speed.

I think three wedges will work for the amateur as well. In general, most amateurs who carry two wedges would be better off taking a long iron out of their bags and adding a third wedge. One key is to make sure all three serve a purpose. The lofts should not be spaced too close or too far apart. For example, if your pitching wedge has 48 degrees of loft, a 54-degree sand wedge and a 60-degree lob wedge would offer consistent spacing. The spacing doesn't have to be exact, but you want to avoid having, say, a 47-degree pitching wedge and a 58-degree sand wedge. That's too big a gap, and adding a 60-degree lob wedge wouldn't give you anything substantially different from your sand wedge.

You also want the bounce on each club to be distinct. Bounce is the feature in wedges that allows the club to slip though sand without digging in. A club's bounce is determined by how much lower the back of the flange is than the leading edge; the lower the back of the flange, the more bounce, and the more easily it will glide through normal, dry sand. While a lot of bounce can make sand shots easier, it makes hitting from the fairway difficult because the back of the flange hits the ground before the leading edge.

Generally, pitching wedges have minimal bounce, sand wedges a lot, and lob wedges something in between. This makes each club suited to a particular purpose inside 60 yards. The pitching wedge will produce shots that fly lower and run more, making it a good club into the wind, or when there is a lot of green between the ball and the pin. The sand wedge can be used from the fairway if it isn't a model with a lot of bounce, or if there is enough grass under the ball that the flange won't hit the ground behind the ball. It produces a shot that will fly higher and carry more spin than the pitching wedge. The lob wedge is made to be a fairway club first, because its minimal bounce won't affect impact on a tight lie. It evolved because the amount of bounce on sand wedges was making it difficult for pros to hit spinning shots from the tighter lies that modern agronomy and course maintenance made possible. The lob wedge makes it easier to hit high shots that spin a lot and land softly. It can also be a good bunker club on short shots, when the sand is firm and the lie is good.

Having three wedges increases a player's options. It also makes it easier to hit different shots without making radical changes in technique. The lob wedge in particular takes a lot of the risk out of short shots to tight pins, which used to require opening the blade on a sand wedge or pitching wedge and cutting across the ball with a glancing blow. With the lob wedge, a standard setup and swing will produce a high shot that lands softly.

What's important is understanding and getting familiar with what each wedge can do, and matching them so they complement, not duplicate, each other. If you do put a lob wedge in your bag, make sure you find the maximum distance you can hit it comfortably—which will probably be about 50 yards—and don't exceed it. If you don't play a lot or practice much, having three wedges can be confusing on shots closer to the green, where you may lack a feel for the differences between the lob wedge and the sand wedge. The only cure for this is to hit more shots and pay attention to the results.

Devote at least 50 percent of practice to the short game

When I joined the tour, most players devoted about 80 percent of their practice time to the long game and 20 percent to the short game. Today, that ratio has been nearly reversed.

It's simple: The more you intelligently practice your short-game skills, the more you'll groove the correct movements, and the better your mind and body will react instinctively to the specific demands of each shot on the course. After getting a good grasp of the fundamentals of setup and swing, repetition of basic chipping, pitching, and sand play is what builds short-game skills. The more you practice, the better you'll understand how lie, ground, slope, and wind affect the ball.

Practice is also how you develop touch and feel. Sure, some people are born with more coordination and tactile skills than others. But with practice, your touch and feel for the shots around the green will increase dramatically.

Besides grooving on the correct movements, practice sessions on the short game should be creative. I think it's important to hit as many different shots from around the green as possible. It's really an area where you can discover a lot of things for yourself: how the ball reacts from different lies, how it reacts when the blade angle is changed, how it reacts with a low, long follow-through as opposed to a quick, short follow-through. With the short game, you can do this on the course, but you can also do it in your backyard or even your hallway. I still do it in hotel rooms.

As a kid growing up in North Carolina with access to my dad's golf course, I would fill hours chipping and pitching on the nearest green, or making the bunkers a little deeper with long sessions in the sand. I don't remember ever being bored. Even then, I got a kick out of experimenting and working the ball and inventing shots, whether it was pinching it, cutting it, punching it, or rolling it. I liked the variety and the magic of it. When I got out on tour and saw short-game wizards like Bob Rosburg, Doug Ford, and Phil Rodgers, I realized there was more magic to discover.

A good way to make short-game practice both fun and purposeful is to practice with a partner. I did this all the time when my sons were growing up. We might each hit three pitches from 30 yards, with the player who did the worst having to pick up the balls. Playing "closest to the hole" against a friend with any short-game shot, perhaps for a small wager, is a good way to learn focus. One game I like for trying lots of different shots is a variation of basketball's H-O-R-S-E, where one player picks the shot, and the player who ends up farther away gets a letter, with the loser the first to spell the word. You'll find yourself trying all sorts of shots in this game.

In golf, we often look for standardization, but really, no two shots are exactly the same, and this goes especially for the short game. If you practice with a purpose, paying attention to good form and doing your best on every shot, you'll begin to realize that almost every shot requires a little improvisation. As you get better at "seeing" the right shot, you'll adjust more naturally to different shots, different stances, and different lies. Practice makes the short game instinctive.

Putting with loft

I've always had a knack for chipping. When I was playing the regular tour, I would average one chip-in per tournament, and I had a few where I holed four or five. I think one of the reasons is that I don't consider it chipping; what most people call chipping, I call *putting with loft.*

I also call it pretty simple. To me, a chip shot from a clean lie is simply a putt with a lofted club. I utilize the same grip, stance, ball position, and stroke that I do with my putter. I simply vary my club selection according to the length of the shot and the ratio of carry to roll that my mind's eye calculates. My standard rule about the best technique for chipping is "like you putt."

Generally, I putt with loft when I'm within 10 feet of the green and I have a shot that will be more effective if it rolls farther than it flies.

Personally, I think the chip from a good lie is the easiest shot in golf. I stand a little closer to the ball than I would on a full shot, so I can better emulate my putting stroke. My feet are open to the target to get my hips out of the way of the stroke, and so I can see my line better. Using an uncomplicated, relaxed swing of the arms and shoulders, it's easy to sweep the ball off the turf from a good lie. I favor a grip pressure that I think of as between firm and light, and there is little hand or body action in the stroke. I try to make sure the right hand doesn't pass the left on the follow-through. I've found that most good chippers reach impact with the back of their left hand slightly ahead of the ball.

The overall stroke should be a crisp but quiet action with a smooth tempo. You don't want any quick flashes of movement when chipping, which can lead to stubbing the club behind the ball or hitting the ball too hard. If you practice and stay relaxed over the ball, it isn't hard to consistently hit the ball solid and approximately the right distance. Learning the chipping motion is probably one of the most productive things beginning golfers can do, because it's essentially a mini-swing that can serve as a foundation for the bigger movements they'll learn later.

Basically, the principle in putting with loft is to keep the ball close to the ground. For most people, it's easier to judge roll than it is to judge flight, and getting the ball rolling requires a simpler, less fallible stroke.

To do this, I don't limit myself to one favorite club for my chip shots around the green. Depending on the shot, I try to take the least-lofted club that will carry the ball onto the putting surface and roll the rest of the way to the hole. The less loft on the club, the shorter I can make my stroke and the less effort I have to use.

It's vital that you have a good feel for how far the ball will roll with each club. A good way to determine this is to practice by chipping so your ball carries to a predetermined spot, then see how far the ball rolls. I find that when chipping with a pitching wedge, the ball rolls roughly twice as far as it carries in the air. With a 5-iron, the lowest-lofted club I chip with, the ball will carry about 10 percent of the distance and roll the remaining 90 percent.

When the ball is in a tight lie, soling the club with the toe slightly down really helps promote clean contact. Less of the leading edge contacts the ground, making it easier to avoid a fat shot, which is death on chips. Finally, a toe hit can slightly deaden impact, if you're worried about a particularly touchy chip.

The less the ball is sitting up in the grass, the farther back in the stance you should play it to create a more descending blow. Grass between club and ball is an enemy on chips, so on hairier lies, the shot will react better if it's "trapped" with a downward blow more than swept.

Once you have a sound, confident method, your success on the course will depend on your ability to visualize—allowing yourself to take the shot into your computer and let your body react. Most bad chips are caused by freezing up and not trusting what your brain has told you. In the worst case, this causes the "chip yips," which I've seen afflict even some tour players. You have to trust yourself.

Naturally, you'll have to judge your growing proficiency in chipping relative to the level of the rest of your game. If you're a high handicapper, your goal should be to get every chip within 10 feet and never take more than three from the edge. For a good player, it's rarely taking more than two. Reach these goals, and you'll be delighted with how your scores will come down.

Today's multilevel greens have made putting with loft more demanding than it used to be, but they've also made it more interesting. With so many slopes and bumps, you have to be very conscious of where you land your shot. Whenever possible, pick the club that will land the ball on a flat area of the green.

By the way, I hole more chips when I take the pin out than when I leave it in. I know studies have shown the opposite, but I just seem to focus better when all I see is the hole. In fact, whenever I chip, I'm trying to hole the shot. That kind of positive attitude can only help your game.

Pitching

The pitch differs from the chip in that it's hit with a wedge from a longer distance, flies higher, and stops quicker. You use it when you have to carry a shot close to the pin and have it stop fairly quickly, which defines the great majority of shots from 20 to 60 yards from the green.

To me, the pitch is the prettiest shot in the game. When great wedge players find a groove, they can hit their pitches stiff time after time. And while there's a uniformity built on fundamentals in their swing action, the trajectory, spin, and even curve of the ball is always customized to the conditions.

In many ways, the pitch shot is *the* scoring shot in golf. To a master of the pitch, there's no pin that isn't accessible. By being able to attack the flag from 60 yards and in, a reasonably good striker of the ball has the capacity to save par on any hole, or birdie any par 5. A golfer who is a great pitcher can always play to his strength, because nearly every golf hole has a place to set up for a basic pitch shot.

The best example of this I ever saw was Billy Casper at the Masters. Just about everything about Billy's long game was wrong for Augusta National: He didn't hit the ball great distances; his ball flight was low; and his predominant curve in his prime was a fade, which runs counter to the shape of most of the holes of Augusta. He rarely went for the short par 5s on the back nine in two. But Billy was a superb wedge player, and he found a way to get into his scoring zone and make a lot of birdies. He contended at the Masters often, and he finally won in 1970. Doug Ford, who won the Masters in 1957, was an even shorter hitter than Casper, and Doug may have been the best pitcher of the ball I ever saw.

The pitch is also a mini-golf swing. Practicing pitch shots that are swept off the turf ingrains a controlled tempo and the correct angle of attack, which will carry over into your full shots. In other words, if you're a good pitcher, you have the foundation to be a good striker throughout the entire bag. Practicing the pitch will improve your whole game.

The pitch is exactly what it says it is. Basically, the motion and the force involved is very similar to tossing a ball underhanded to the target. To calculate the distance, I think of having the ball in my hand and tossing it fairly high up to the hole. It's a rhythmic movement, and the club is simply an extension of the arms.

It's not a complicated action, and the simpler you can keep it, the better. I stand a little open to the target, both to get my hips out of the way of my arm swing and to see the target better. During the swing, there is obviously more body action than in executing a chip, but it's mostly just the rocking of the knees creating a subtle weight shift. I find that keeping my right foot on the ground during the follow-through helps me stay very solid on the shot.

From a good lie, don't take much of a divot for a standard pitch shot. Sweeping the ball off the turf facilitates clean contact, produces plenty of backspin, and launches the ball at the proper height. A shot that's swept off the turf is easier to control than one that produces a big divot because the arc of the swing is shallower in the impact area. A sharp descending blow can create more backspin, but if the contact isn't flush, it makes distance and trajectory control a problem.

I used to hit almost all my pitches with a 56-degree sand wedge. The only problem with that club is that from tight lies, the built-in "bounce" behind the leading edge of the blade can strike the ground first, inhibiting clean contact. Like a lot of players, in recent years I've begun carrying a 60-degree lob wedge with less bounce that's specifically designed for these shots. If you find you like the lob wedge for pitches, beware of hitting your shots too high, or trying to hit the shot too far. A nice, compact swing will produce a manageable trajectory and distance control.

Chip or pitch?

As we've seen, there are general situations that suit each type of shot. But a great many shots—especially those that don't call for carrying over a bunker, water, or rough—can legitimately be played either way. This is where your own personal aptitude and preferences come to the forefront. I know I like to get the ball on the ground and rolling most of the time, so I prefer chipping. It seems that many young players who grew up with the 60-degree wedge like to fly the ball most of the way to the hole whenever they can, sometimes more often than they should. An interesting combination is Dave Stockton, a superb short-game player who uses his sand wedge almost exclusively around the greens. But Dave knows how to hit every kind of shot with that club, from running chips to high lobs.

You'll probably be better at one or the other. Find where your knack lies, and then follow your instincts.

A couple of guidelines. As always, the lie of the ball dictates what's possible. While you'll have plenty of options from a good lie, difficult lies call for more specific strategies. From thin lies or when the ball is sitting down on tight ground, running the ball low with a trapping action of the clubhead is best. From higher grass, a pitching action in which a wedge gets more under the ball makes the most sense. When hitting into an uphill green from inside 60 yards, I favor a lower, more rolling shot, because the bank eats up any shot with backspin and forces you to fly the ball farther. The same goes when there is a heavy wind; even when I'm downwind, if I've got plenty of green to work with I like to hit a lower shot that won't get blown around as much and that runs up to the hole. On hard, fast greens where you have green to work with, a rolling ball will react more predictably than one that's flown farther with backspin.

Another word of warning: Most amateurs tend to be partial to flying the ball because of the neat way the ball responds to backspin. This is the wrong reason to choose a shot. Rolling the ball to the target is an easier shot to execute, especially when you get a little tense. Because it's a shorter swing, less can go wrong. Sometimes the perfect shot would be a pitch or lob of some sort, but the percentage shot is a chip. Pretty is as pretty does.

On the other hand, even if you feel most comfortable getting the ball rolling along the ground, avoid doing it when the ground in front of the green has heavy grass, or will produce uneven bounces. Fly the ball farther instead, particularly if the green is soft and holds a shot well.

Sand play

If you want to be a scorer, you have to learn to make sand shots what they truly are: fairly simple shots with a large margin for error.

Unlike so many amateurs, pros find sand play a place where they have a lot of ball control. Pros actually prefer playing from bunkers over green-side rough because a ball will react more predictably and is easier to control from sand than from long grass. It's not unusual to hear a pro who's hit a wayward approach call out, "Get in the trap!"

This is the opposite of many amateurs, for whom the bunker is their worst fear. But like many fears, it's born of ignorance. That fear will disappear when you understand how a bunker shot works —and when you do, you'll never again have trouble getting the ball out of the bunker. With some practice, you'll find yourself actually getting the ball close enough to one-putt.

It's really very simple: If you can slip your sand wedge completely under the ball and follow through, the ball will come out—high, soft-landing, and with spin. You're basically tossing a handful of sand out of the bunker; because the ball is the largest of the grains of sand, it will travel the farthest, which is what you want.

There is actually more margin for error on a green-side sand shot from a good lie than any other shot. On green-side sand shots of less than 40 yards, the club never even touches the ball; all you have to do is displace the sand around the ball. If you try to contact the sand three inches behind the ball, and instead contact it four inches or two inches behind, as long as the club continues under the ball you'll still hit a serviceable shot.

Slipping the club under is no problem if you understand the dynamics of the sand wedge. Bounce allows the club to skim along just below the surface of the sand without digging in deeply, creating a thin cushion of sand that will propel the ball out.

Experimenting with the bounce on the sand wedge will make you a better sand player. Basically, laying the face open activates the bounce, and the best way to do this is to align your feet so that your left foot is well back from your right, and then open the face approximately 35 degrees until it's aligned with the target. It's also helpful to have your hands slightly behind the ball to ensure that the flange contacts the sand first. From this setup, it's simply a matter of making a slightly outside-to-in swing that allows the club to skim under the sand. I like to think of the club as a flat rock skipping along the water. The longer I can keep the bottom of that club skimming, the easier it is to hit a good shot.

It's important that the clubhead not turn over and close through impact, which destroys the bounce effect and causes the clubhead to dig. To ensure that this doesn't happen, don't apply your normal grip with the clubface square and then turn the face open; instead, open the face first, and then apply your grip as you would if the club were square. On the forward swing, resist letting the right hand turn over.

To be a good sand player, you want the sensation of thumping the sand with the bottom of the flange. Some veterans describe it as spanking the sand. I can always tell a good sand player by the deep "thump" sound his shots make.

Spin is produced through clubhead speed, and by how close to the ball the face slips through the sand on a clean lie. The closer to the ball, the more spin (because the sand is moving faster against the ball); the farther, the more the ball will come out dead (because the sand is moving more slowly against the ball). Different sand produces different results: In firm sand, the ball will fly farther with less effort and will spin more because of the greater friction. Softer sand requires more effort to hit the ball the same distance, and the ball will have less spin, so it will roll more when it lands. In firm sand, like we generally have on the professional tours, the 60-degree wedge with minimal bounce generally works well. Out of soft sand, like the silica-based sand found in Florida, a club with more bounce is useful. Try to allow some time in the practice bunker as part of your standard pre-round warmup to get used to the type of sand you'll be facing. (Still, because the consistency of sand on a course can vary from bunker to bunker, you should train yourself to feel the sand through your shoes as you dig in at address.)

I like to vary the distance I hit sand shots more with the speed and angle of the clubhead than with the distance I hit behind the ball, which stays pretty constant between two and three inches behind the ball.

Naturally, adjustments have to be made for buried or semi-buried lies. But the basic principle remains the same: If the club goes under the ball, it will come out. If you have to dig deep, the bounce of the club can work against you, so opening the clubhead less will extract a ball more easily from a buried lie. But because balls hit from buried lies will carry almost no backspin, a shot with a closed-down face will come out hotter. Opening the face produces a softer shot, but runs the risk of not getting the club under the ball.

You will find all sorts of variables to green-side sand shots, but once you master the basic principle of using the sand wedge's design properly, you'll start to consider sand shots fun and an interesting challenge. Besides being able to apply a lot of spin and height to your shots, with practice you can achieve great control.

When you see your ball go into a bunker, you'll start to relish the opportunity to pull off a shot in which the ball behaves like it does for no other shot in the game.

Don't be seduced by spin

Almost all shots have some degree of backspin. If you're playing intelligently, a little backspin goes a long way. That's why I rarely try to hit wedge shots that spin more than normal unless it's the only way I can get close to the pin. If you're fascinated by these shots where the ball spins back after it hits, you should realize that the pursuit of spin can easily lead you to trying low-percentage shots and cause bad habits in your technique.

Pros can spin the ball with their wedges because of several factors. First and foremost, we generate plenty of clubhead speed, and we hit the ball cleanly and solidly. The balls we play have a soft cover and spin much more than the hard-cover balls many amateurs play. And pros also play under ideal conditions to create spin: Firm, lush fairways allow us to really nip the ball off the turf, so that when a pitch of 60 yards or so lands on a fast but not overly firm green, the ball either stops very quickly or even spins backward.

It's important to understand the conditions that produce spin. Assuming clean contact, the ball will always spin more from the fairway than the rough, always spin more into the wind than with it, always spin more with a soft-cover ball than with a hard-cover ball, always spin more with a higher-lofted club than a lower one, and will stop more quickly on a soft green than a firm one.

There are times when a lot of spin is advantageous or necessary, of course; there's nothing like a high spinner to get the ball to stop near a tight pin or on a very firm green. If you have the skills, go ahead and hit it, although it's important to understand that trying to put extra spin on a shot almost always increases the margin for error. But if you can't spin the ball a lot, compensate by playing intelligent angles, or in certain cases playing a safer shot away from the pin.

If it's any comfort, even a touring pro couldn't back the ball up on a worn-out muni with baked greens. Be content with the amount of spin you can generate by hitting the ball solidly. Most times, seeking a lot of spin is unnecessary and just makes golf harder than it needs to be.

Wind and the short game

It might not seem like it should, but wind has a profound effect on pitches and even chips. Backspin is increased into the wind, which means that not only will the ball travel a shorter distance in the air, it will stop faster and perhaps even spin back. With the wind, backspin is decreased, so along with the greater distance the ball will travel in the air, it will also roll farther forward once it lands. A crosswind will influence the ball on chips and pitches; if it's strong, it will bend the ball so that when it lands it will roll at an angle rather than straight. Make a significant allowance for crosswinds, especially on fast, firm greens. The faster the green, the more the wind can push the ball in its direction.

A head wind can be your ally, especially when you want to stop the ball fast. Downwind, short shots are more difficult because the extra run of the ball has to be calculated. In general, flighting the ball lower in the wind makes it easier to control.

Most amateurs tend to underestimate the effect of wind on the short game. Scorers don't.

The toughest short-game shots

There are some short-game shots that are hard for everyone, no matter how accomplished a player you are.

The long bunker shot from about 50 or 60 yards from the pin is in my opinion the hardest shot in golf. You're too far away to hit behind the ball with a sand wedge, too close to hit a full shot by picking it clean, and it's very difficult to judge how far the ball will go. There are two basic ways to play it: One is to grip down on your sand wedge, hold it lightly, position the ball in the center of your stance, and pick the ball off the sand by hitting the ball first. The other is to take a longer club, like a 7- or 8-iron, and hit a mini-explosion shot, striking the sand an inch or so behind the ball. Open the blade slightly, and cut across the ball from outside to in; the ball will fly out lower than with a normal explosion and spin from left to right. You need a good lie to hit this shot—and plenty of practice. Try them both, and find out which is more reliable for you.

The flop shot from rough takes judgment, touch, and nerve. When the ball is down in high grass, you've got to swing relatively hard to get it moving, but still produce a shot that lands on the green softly. Trying to determine how a ball will come out of high grass is always a bit of a guessing game, so it's easy to either leave the ball in the rough or have it fly too far and go well past the hole. The best club for this shot is a lob wedge, and the technique is similar to a sand shot. Aim at a point a couple of inches behind the ball and make the same swing as you would in the sand. If you need the ball to come out high and soft, open the face and slide it under the ball. Unlike the sand shot, a green-side flop shot from rough will carry next to no backspin. The best you can do is to hit a very soft shot to minimize the run.

The bump shot is one you might face when you've missed an elevated green on the sides or long, with the pin cut close to the fringe. Rather than try a soft-cut shot, a better play is to hit a low shot into the bank and let it bounce softly onto the green. This shot is most effective when the ground on the bank is firm and the grass is low. It's a tough shot to judge precisely, and there's the chance of leaving the ball in the bank and having it roll back to you. If you're going to err, do so on the long side rather than the short.

The bunker shot from a severe downhill lie can be very dangerous. The most important element is to make sure that your shoulders run parallel to the ground. Play the ball more back in your stance, pick the club up more abruptly and swing down along the slope, making extra sure to get the clubhead under the ball. Because the slope is going away from you, it's harder to keep the club under the ball: To counteract this, try to make the club enter the sand closer to the ball than on a normal sand shot—about two inches or less. The ball will come out lower and roll farther when it hits the green. This is a shot that is equally easy to mishit heavily or thinly. The priority for the scorer is getting the ball out of the bunker and onto the green, hopefully within 20 feet of the hole. But even if you can't get it close, out of the bunker is still better than in.

Having to hit off hardpan over a bunker from inside 30 yards of the green leaves no margin for error on a conventional pitch; its very easy to blade the ball or chunk it. I think the best shot here is an explosion with a sand wedge, hitting close behind the ball with a firm swing. Because the ground is firm, the club must hit within an inch of the ball, and you have to make sure you drive the clubhead under the ball. The ball will come out lower than a sand shot, but it will carry some backspin.

Before trying any of these unusual shots during a round, become familiar with them in practice.

There's nothing wrong with putting

It's often said about shots from the fringe that "your worst putt is better than your worst chip," and for most golfers it's true. I still believe that a good chipping technique that will fly the ball onto the green is more reliable than putting over bumpy or hairy fringe, but there are times when putting from off the green makes more sense than chipping—when the ball is very close to the green, the fringe is very smooth, the lie is very thin, and/or the putting surface is very fast. It's important that the speed the ball will roll on the fringe not be dramatically slower than it will be on the green, as that makes it very difficult to determine how hard to hit the ball. Putting is generally a sound choice on such shots of more than 30 feet, because a firmly hit putt will actually go in the air slightly after impact and be affected less by fringe. Another time to use your putter is if you suffer a loss of confidence with your chipping; if you feel you can't get the job done with a lofted club but can with a putter, go with the flat stick. Then be sure to practice your chipping after the round.

The effect of the ball

There are many different types of balls on the market today. Generally, the harder two-piece balls will go farther, but they also spin less. That makes them harder to control in the short game. They land "hot," and if the hole is on a slope or near a ledge, a hard ball makes a finesse shot extremely difficult no matter how good your technique. Professionals use soft-cover balls with a high spin rate, in large part so they can control the short shots. If you're a short hitter, a harder-cover ball may make the most sense for you, but be aware that the softer the ball, the more you can do with it around the greens.

Chapter 8

Putting

*I*f you're going to be a scorer, you have to be a good putter. Putting has more effect on score than any other area of the game. Even pros take an average of 43 percent of their shots on the greens. And in golf, the shortest shots are the most important.

There's no way around it—a missed short putt is final. A sprayed drive, a wayward approach, even a poor pitch or chip is to some extent salvageable with a good putt—or as Walter Hagen used to say, "three of these and one of those still make four." But a missed putt from within 6 feet is a stroke lost.

If I could be the best at anything in the game, it would be putting. I consider putting a high calling, a combination of skill, mental toughness, and intelligence. Unlike some of my peers, I'm proud to be considered, and more important, to consider myself, a good putter. You're only hurting yourself if you don't have an ultrapositive attitude about putting. The PGA Tour is full of great ball strikers who seldom win because they're mediocre putters; it's also full of mediocre ball strikers who win quite often because they are tremendous putters.

Putting, more than any other area of the game, is definitely art, not science. It's been proven that even a machine, perfectly calibrated for speed and line, misses 6-footers. As we noted before, pros make only about 50 percent of them. Jack Nicklaus, probably the best clutch putter ever, said that putting is really the one place in golf where you have to give in to luck; if you try to force the ball into the hole, you'll only get worse. You just have to hit the best putt you can, and submit to fate. Up to the moment of impact, you've got to believe you will make the putt. But once the putt is struck, you've got to fully accept a miss. Let yourself get lost in the process of hitting good putts, rather than anxiety about the result, and it will take the pressure off.

If there is one constant I've found for being successful on the greens, it's that good putters believe they are good putters. Simple as that. They can miss ten 3-footers in a row, and they will still say they are good putters. Good putters keep believing in themselves; for them, the opportunity to succeed overwhelms the fear of failure. Having that belief is the greatest attribute you can have on the greens. I'm convinced that, after seeing so many different types of styles be successful, putting more than anything is *attitude*.

To be a good putter, it's important to enjoy the act of putting. Some very good players don't. As much as I respected Ben Hogan, I think he hurt himself late in his career by being very dismissive of putting, considering it far inferior to the challenge of ball-striking. He would even play a competition among his friends in which there was no putting, just points for fairways and greens hit and closest to the hole. What gets to a lot of players is the seeming absurdity of a 2-foot putt counting as much as a well-struck 210-yard approach shot over water, especially when the 2-foot putt is missed. It's this resentment of putting's importance that is at the root of the fear of short putts, which is what causes what are commonly known as "the yips."

I'm fortunate to have always enjoyed putting. To me, it's both athletic and creative. I also look at the ability to hole putts at the right time as the ultimate test of whether a player has what it takes to be a winner. As a teenager, I learned what it's like to have to make a 5-footer with more than you can afford to lose riding on it. Even then, something was telling me that as much as it was making my mouth dry and my stomach tight, I had better *want* those situations if I was going to be successful. I learned to look at those occasions as opportunities to get better, as challenges I couldn't back away from, and I've drawn on those experiences ever since. Whenever I had a chance to make a putt to win a tournament, my feeling was that this was what it was all about, so I relished the opportunity. If I failed, I still considered myself lucky to have had the chance. Even after thirty-five years of playing for pay, I love seeing that little white pellet tracking toward the hole.

Great putters are self-made

Putting is the most individual aspect of golf, and finding something that works, and sticking with it, is key. The great putters in history have employed countless different methods. There are so many ways to do it, and the best have always trusted their individual methods.

There's an old saying: "The best way to putt is the way you putt best." If you find a method that works, by all means, keep doing it.

The three constants

For all the differences, I think there are three constants: All good putters have a consistent routine. All good putters are comfortable. And, on short- to medium-length putts, all good putters stay still during the stroke.

As we've seen, routine is important because it's where the mind hones in. It's where a golfer can eliminate every thought except hitting the best putt he can and rolling the ball in the hole. If your routine is truly ingrained, you'll be able to treat the biggest putt of your life as if it were a practice putt, even if you're as nervous as a cat.

With the best putters, the movements preceding and during the stroke are identical, and the time elapsed from the moment they take their stance to the moment of impact doesn't vary.

How do you develop such a routine? Through thoughtful practice. Pay attention to your habits, and keep the ones that serve a purpose and make you feel comfortable. I do believe you'll putt better if you make your routine efficient and economical. Taking a lot of time is usually counterproductive, and fidgety movements are best eliminated if you can. Although I'm deliberate on the greens, I like to feel that there's a flow to my movements that keeps me from freezing or losing my concept of the speed and line.

In developing your routine during practice, be disciplined. Don't hit aimless putts. Pretend you're putting to win the U.S. Open or your club championship, and carry that same focus on all your putts. The point, as much as possible, is to make every putt the same.

The second thing that good putters are is comfortable, even when they get into some seemingly uncomfortable positions. Arnold Palmer may have seemed contorted in his pigeon-toed stance, but when he putted, he looked so solid you just knew the putt was going in. Jack Nicklaus crouched low behind the ball and held the position for a very long time, but his action was graceful.

Although I believe in an orthodox posture and alignment on full shots, it's more important to be comfortable when putting than to have the body perfectly aligned. There are putting gurus who swear by a stance in which an imaginary line through the feet, hips, and shoulders makes them all parallel to the target line; such a stance probably does facilitate correct aim for most people, but some of the best putters I know, like Ben Crenshaw, Brad Faxon, and Jack Nicklaus, stand open to the target. I've always stood a little open because I feel it helps me see the line better as I prepare to hit the putt. On the other hand, Bobby Locke, maybe the best putter who ever lived, stood closed. So does Gary Player.

What's important is that the putter swing in a way that's relaxed, repeatable, and consistently along the target line, and that happens most easily when you're comfortable.

Grip pressure can also give you comfort. I say the way I hold the putter is "secure," neither light nor tight. A lot of very good putters use very light grip pressure. But I know Tom Watson has always used very firm grip pressure. Again, let comfort be your guide.

When a player is putting badly, one of the most common reasons he'll give is that he just doesn't feel comfortable. The best solution, rather than searching for a correction in the stroke or alignment, is often to simply find a stance that's more comfortable and go from there.

I switched to a longer putter in 1975 because it helped me feel more comfortable. My 35-inch-long putter forced me to bend over a lot, and long practice sessions started causing me a lot of pain in my lower back. I went to a 38-inch putter so I could stand straighter and more relaxed, which eliminated the pain. I've been a better putter ever since.

My third absolute is that good putters stay still over the ball. The only exception is on long putts, in which the bigger swing causes the body to move involuntarily.

On shorter putts, the biggest single reason for missing them is moving before impact, especially by peeking with the head. We've all seen short putts missed under pressure: Doug Sanders's missed 3-footer on the seventy-second hole of the 1970 British Open was a classic example of peeking. In the wind, it's especially important to be conscious of being still, because a strong breeze will sway the body.

I've found a simple gimmick to help me stay still during the stroke. I line up the trademark of the ball so that it's where the face of my putter will make contact. Then, when I'm over the putt, I stare that trademark down until the putter contacts that precise spot. Keeping my eyes that focused seems to steady my whole body.

Reading greens

A scorer has to be able to read a putt. In the most basic terms, this means calculating the effects of slope, speed, grain, and wind on each putt. In ultimate terms, it means being able to put aside all calculations and actually "feel" the ball into the hole.

There are a few rules to keep in mind. A putt will always break more as it starts to slow down than when it's traveling faster. This means that most putts will break more in their second half than they do in the first, when they have the most momentum from leaving the club. Given the same slope, a putt will always

THE ELEMENTS OF SCORING

break more on a fast green than on a slow green. A putt will fall in the sides of a hole more easily the more slowly it's traveling.

Generally, putts break away from mountains and toward water. As you approach a green from the fairway, take in the lay of the land. It's not a hard-and-fast rule, but greens tend to break toward the surrounding low spots, because they're built for drainage. When in doubt, I allow my imagination to work for me: When I have some question about the slope of the terrain, I imagine emptying a bucket of water along the line of my putt, and watching where the water would drain.

It's true that most people underread break. I'm not sure why this is, but Dave Pelz, who has made a specialty of teaching the short game, believes that almost everyone would be better off allowing for twice as much break as they see.

I think part of it is that golfers fail to understand that break increases as the ball slows—so if a putt you played for 3 inches of break dies at the hole, it's likely to break 6 inches in the last 2 feet.

If you have any doubt about how much a putt is going to break, err toward the high side. As long as the ball is above the cup when it starts to die, it has a chance of going in. It also has more of the cup to catch if it's coming in high and from the side, rather than low and from the front.

Also, your chances of making a putt are better if your speed is such that the ball is dying at the hole. It gives the putt a chance not only to go in the front of the hole, but the side entrances and the back door as well; "dying" the putt effectively gives you a wider hole. However, a putt that is dying is also more likely to wander off line, so there are some putts—especially short, straight ones —that are better attacked by putting firmly for the back of the cup.

Grass never grows straight up, which means there is grain in every green. The longer and coarser the grass, like Bermuda, the more the ball will be affected by the grain. A putt traveling in the direction of the grain will roll faster and farther; one going against the grain will roll slower and not as far. When the grain is running across on a level putt, the ball will break in the direction of the grain. Grain can be so prominent that it can sometimes make a ball break uphill.

Grain tends to grow along the direction of a slope, or the way that water runs off the green. Again, in general, Bermuda grass tends to lay down toward the setting sun, which is why otherwise straight putts on Bermuda tend to break to the west. The texture and color of the grass is also an indicator of the direction of the grain: When you look downgrain, the putting surface will appear lighter and have a sheen to it. Upgrain, the grass will appear darker and coarser.

Wind can also dramatically affect how a putt moves, especially on fast greens. A downwind, downgrain putt will seem to roll forever, while an upgrain, uphill putt will seem to slow down prematurely. Wind can also be forceful enough to cause putts to break uphill, or roll off the green on downhill, downgrain putts. The effect is also increased because wind dries out greens.

All these things can be learned through experience and practice. But I want to emphasize that once you're familiar with how physical conditions affect putts, your senses will take in a tremendous amount of information intuitively if you're truly focused on the shot at hand.

In other words, rather than trying to exactly calculate the forces at work on a putt, trust your instincts. I don't think it's an accident that my first read from behind the ball looking toward the hole is usually my best one. It's because my senses have already processed information without my having broken it all down analytically. Often, when I try to get very precise and read a putt by looking at it from more than one side, I get my signals crossed and end up with a confused sense of the line. I do my best when I let myself "feel" the line, allowing my senses to take in information and trusting my instincts to react. When I address the ball, instead of thinking "hit it 3 inches outside the right edge," I let my body align itself according to what it's absorbed. There are times when I "spot" putt—aiming over a mark on the green that's on my line—but I roll more good putts when I allow my feel to take over.

A large part of reading greens is simply trusting your instincts. I honestly believe you're better off with the wrong read with a lot of confidence than with the right read but a lot of doubt. There is something about a strong, competitive will that seems to make the ball go in. No matter your approach, indecision is a killer.

Short putts

Some putts are more important than others, and the most important of all are inside 6 feet. If you make them, it means your stroke is solid, which builds confidence for longer putts. It also means you can go at longer putts aggressively, knowing you can make the comebackers.

Conversely, missing them regularly makes it impossible to shoot a low score and causes your momentum to not only stop but —unless you are *very* strong mentally—go backward. There is nothing more discouraging in golf than not being able to convert short putts.

The yips develop over a fear of short putts. Because you're supposed to make them, it's easy to believe that when putting them you have nothing to gain and everything to lose.

That's the wrong attitude. First, you have to accept that there is nothing automatic about short putts; to make them takes good technique, concentration, and discipline. Even when all those things are adhered to, the odd one is going to lip out. Accepting that there is difficulty in what you're doing should lessen your fear of failure.

That doesn't mean you should take misses lying down. You *should* make most of your short putts. But you have to pay the price. That means practice.

Personally, I think there's no better practice than hitting a lot of short putts in a competitive frame of mind. That can mean participating in putting games for some small wager, or simply using your imagination to simulate a competitive situation. It's the best way to lessen fear and build confidence.

Gary Player has a drill in which he tries to make 100 straight from 2 feet, with the proviso that he has to start at zero if he misses at any point. Believe me, it's not easy, and the pressure really builds. The drill accomplishes three things: It gets Gary used to watching the ball go into the hole; it steels him against the fear of missing short ones, which every player feels at some point; and it helps him groove his stroke. (For the average player, 25 straight is probably tough enough to be helpful.)

I know a lot of players who don't like to hit short putts before a round because they're afraid that a few misses will cost them their confidence, but I think this is backward thinking. If you're missing, you have an opportunity to straighten out what is probably just poor concentration before it can hurt you during the round.

Consistently making short putts takes discipline, toughness, concentration, and the right attitude. Never take them for granted.

The crucial 6- to 10-foot putt

Missing short putts can ruin your score. But the putts that can make or break a great round are those that are slightly longer, in the 6- to 10-foot range. Very often they're putts to save par after missing the green, but it really doesn't matter what the putt is for —when you make one, it feels like you stole a stroke, and when you miss one, you know you've wasted an opportunity. Just as a tennis match has big points, the 6- to 10-foot putt is often a crucial stroke.

It's important to remember the real odds on these putts. Pros barely make half of their 6-footers, and about only one in three 10-footers. The rate for amateurs is obviously even lower. This means that when you face such a putt, be realistic. This will let you relax before you make the stroke, and help you accept failure without losing your cool.

Still, it seems to me that scorers are very good at making these putts at crucial junctures in the round. People who thrive on competition seem to bear down in a positive way on this length putt. These are the putts on which a solid stroke, a clear mind, and a strong will really pay off.

When I face such a putt, I try to keep things simple. I usually avoid mechanical thoughts, following Jack Burke's dictum that "bad putting stems from thinking how instead of where." I just want to hit the putt as solidly as I can; when you achieve solid contact, it usually means the putter has swung smoothly and squarely through impact.

Psychologically, I'm trying to see the putt going into the hole before I start the stroke. But I'm also reminding myself that I don't have to hit a perfect putt to make it; good speed will give the ball access to all four doors of the hole—the front, the sides, and the back.

When you face a 6- to 10-foot putt, don't look at it as do or die, but as an opportunity. That will allow you to relax and hit the best putt possible, which is really all you can do.

Long putts

There's a theory that the best way to approach long putts is to try to leave them in an imaginary 3-foot circle around the hole. That was my philosophy until I started playing practice rounds with Arnold Palmer in the early '60s. He seemed to make a lot of long putts, and came awfully close when he missed. One day I asked him, "Arnold, what's your approach to long putts?" He kind of looked at me funny for a second, and finally said, "What do you mean? I try to make 'em all." That hit me as a novel idea, but a good one; I started trying to make them too, and I got better.

It turns out that sports psychologists now endorse this goal. The more specific the target, the better the focus and the better the performance. I know that when Nick Price was on top, he said he was trying to hole everything inside 100 yards. If it works from there, it should certainly work from 60 feet.

A feel for distance is the key to negotiating long putts. That feel comes from practice, but also from allowing your senses to work as you stand over the ball. Look at the hole, feel the path to the hole, and stay relaxed. Then, trusting that you're properly programmed, simply hit a solid putt.

The best example of this in my career occurred in the third round of the 1986 U.S. Open at Shinnecock Hills. On the eighth hole I was struggling, but had managed to get the ball on the green with a 50-foot putt for a birdie. I was really on top of my mental game that week, and as I surveyed the putt, I got a strong feeling that I would make it. When that putt went in, I had no outward reaction for several seconds other than staring at the hole. I was still in the trance that had "felt" that putt into the hole.

Putters: a question of balance

If you can find a putter that looks good behind the ball and has a sweet spot you both like and can hit consistently, you've got a keeper.

There are as many variables in putters as there are styles of putting. They include grip shape and thickness, shaft length and flex, overall weight and swingweight, and loft. Most putters on the market have relatively standard specifications that can be altered by a clubmaker. Preferences are best determined by trial and error.

In recent years, so-called face-balanced putters have become popular. These putters are weighted on the toe and heel to prevent the toe from opening and closing as much during the stroke. I use one myself.

Be careful when switching to such a putter if you've been using a heel-weighted putter. You may find that because the weighting keeps the toe from swinging open, your putter face will be closed relative to what you're used to. Pulled putts are often the result.

If you're wondering about trying the long putter, go ahead. I've never used one in a round, but if I knew I would putt better with one, you can be sure I would. My basic feeling is, if you're putting well, don't change anything. But if you aren't comfortable with a putter, change to something that makes you comfortable and gives you confidence. You will putt better.

How many putts?

How many putts should you take a round? Well, a lot depends on the size, undulation, and condition of the greens you play on; how many greens in regulation you hit; and how good a chipping and pitching game you have. I will say that if you're playing on a course with relatively flat, small- to average-size greens, and you have a good short game, you should definitely average under thirty-five putts a round, and your goal should be to average under thirty.

This is what pros average, and they generally hit between eleven and fifteen greens a round in regulation, which usually leaves them a substantial number of approach putts longer than 30 feet. If you're hitting only six or seven greens in regulation, you should actually have a lot more chances at one-putts than a touring pro has. I know that on tour, when players have bad ball-striking rounds and hit six or seven greens, they often have twenty-three or twenty-four putts.

Get in touch with the child within

When I was a kid spending my summer days around my dad's course in Fort Bragg, I would mess around on the putting green for hours, playing for nickels and dimes; or if I was alone, I'd pretend I was coming down the stretch at Augusta, fighting for the lead.

Perhaps my memory has been altered by nostalgia, but I remember being an incredible putter when I was young. It seemed like I made at least one long putt a round and would handle 5-footers like they were tap-ins. It's something I've noticed with my own sons and others who take up the game young—kids can really putt. They take very little time looking at the line; they just step up and charge it in. It's interesting, because to this day, Ben Crenshaw, who has been the best putter for the longest period over the last twenty-five years, still has moments when he spontaneously gives a putt a cursory look and gets up and holes it. When we putt, we would probably all do better by getting back to the child within.

Be quietly arrogant on the greens

Attitude is the real bottom line in putting. I think one of the best ways to make yourself a good putter is to have what I call "presence" on the greens. Without being obnoxiously demonstrative, be arrogant on the greens. Relish your opportunity to putt. When it's your turn, you're on stage. Perform.

You can usually tell a good putter by the ease of his movements, the graceful way he walks on the green, the rhythm of his stroke. Bad putters are jerky, hesitant. I always get the feeling with really good putters that they have the grace of a pool shark running the table. Ben Crenshaw is beautiful on the greens, and so is Corey Pavin. Watch how the best do it, and try to move like a player.

This is the key to pressure putting: wanting it. Looking at it as an opportunity. And understanding that something is not really fun unless it's also a little scary.

Remember and call upon good experiences on the greens. I call this "memory banking," and it's important when you've succeeded to relish the experience so that it becomes vivid and easily recalled. Under pressure, past success can provide strength.

So carry yourself with confidence on the greens, even if you've got to pose a little. I like it when, after I've made a putt, someone says to me, "You looked like you were going to make it." That's how I want to look on the greens, and so should you.

Let Your Mind
Feel the Target

I've always considered myself a feel player. As a young golfer I learned by feel, and I've played by feel as a pro. Even as I learned the fundamentals and incorporated swing changes into my game, I've absorbed them through feel.

When we talk about feel in golf, it sounds like we're describing the sensitivity in your hands, but I think it's much broader than that; it actually emanates from the mind. Having an instinct for the game, for shaping shots, for making swing adjustments, for improvisation, for getting the ball into the hole—all the things we associate with feel—come down to how well you allow your brain to process the information you take in before every golf shot. In essence, I'm a feel player because I play golf with my eyes.

Every scorer does this. But while everyone agrees that using imagination and creativity to get around the golf course is an important part of scoring, it's also the part of the game we seem to know the least about. The hunger for more knowledge in this area is one reason so many top players have begun to work with sports psychologists in the last decade.

From my own investigation and experience, I'd sum up the role of the mind in golf with one operative phrase: "getting out of your own way." It means not cluttering up the messages of the brain to the body with a lot of unnecessary information, but rather having simple thoughts and trusting your instinct and the power of the unconscious to guide the body to perform. You have to know enough and observe enough to make the right judgments, but once you've made those judgments you have to put the conscious mind aside and let that knowledge flow through you.

It's what winning athletes do. When Utah Jazz guard John Stockton was recently asked to analyze and describe what he was thinking during a series of game-winning plays he made in the NBA finals against the Chicago Bulls, he said, "I'm not a very cerebral player. I just play basketball." While to some it might have sounded as if Stockton was further reinforcing the stereotype of the dumb jock, he was really doing just the opposite: As a future Hall of Fame point guard, he can probably analyze offensive or defensive schemes and theories as well as any coach, but that's not the kind of thought process he wants to use on the court. While playing, Stockton simply wants to trust his unconscious—which houses all that basketball knowledge—and react. He is smart enough to "just play basketball."

As a scorer, your goal on the course should be to just play golf. Even though golf is a slow game that allows plenty of time to think, from the moment you begin your pre-shot routine, you want a clear mind that is thinking only of the simple task at hand, which is to hit the ball to the target. In this state, the body is relaxed, and the focus is strictly on where—not how—you want to hit the ball. Imagine a very hungry caveman throwing a spear at his prey. I seriously doubt he had any thoughts about his release point or how high to carry his right elbow. I'll bet he was thinking about precisely where he had to throw that spear. If he wasn't "out of his own way," he didn't eat.

I'm not saying golf should be played with a blank mind. Far from it. But rather than having many scattered thoughts, you should have one very focused one. A scorer has control of what he chooses to think of on the golf course. He knows that to a large extent, he is only as good as his thoughts. This chapter is about what those thoughts should be.

The target is everything

Good thoughts start and end with the ultimate object of every golf shot; the target. All the other things golfers are encouraged to think can breed paralysis by analysis; target-oriented golf does the exact opposite. Rather than promote confusion, it induces focus. The more you can become target-aware when you're on the golf course, the better you will play.

When you're thinking only of the target, you're thinking only of the shot at hand and executing it as well as possible. Do that shot after shot, and you're truly playing golf. You'll be doing what the pros call "hitting it where you're looking." It's pure play, the highest state in the game.

When I'm playing my best, I react to the target—the fairway, the green, or the hole—and what it tells me to do. When I'm playing my worst, I can't seem to stop thoughts of where I don't want the ball to go from intruding. Because the body reacts to what the brain thinks, these negative thoughts cause the ball to be hit in precisely that undesirable place. How many times have you seen a water hazard on a hole and thought, "Whatever you do, don't hit it over there." Then, with a clear picture of water in your mind, your ball flew into the hazard as if pulled by a magnet. Actually, the magnet was your thoughts. You want those thoughts directed at the target. There's all the difference in the world between "Hit it left," and "Don't hit it right."

If you want to be a scorer, you have to know how to mentally hone in on the target. That means always having one, whether in practice or on the golf course. By getting used to having a target, your mind will get better at taking in information and at narrowing down its focus. To be a scorer, make your target small: On a tee shot, rather than aiming at a tree in the distance, pick out a limb on that tree. Rather than aiming at the center of the green, aim at a small discoloration on the putting surface. Don't just aim at the flag, but at the bottom of the flag. While putting, aim at the very back of the hole, or the exact blade of grass on the lip that the ball will roll over on its way in. Having small targets increases focus and helps shut out distraction.

All this target projection is done during the pre-shot routine. To illustrate how I focus on the target, I'll walk you through mine.

When I'm within 20 yards of my ball, and often earlier than that, I begin to study what kind of shot I might want to play. When I get to the ball, I get the yardage from my caddy, assess where the pin is, and take in all the factors that will give this shot its own particular character—the lay of the land, the wind, the lie, etc.

After I've chosen a club, I really get focused. I back up to a position about 4 yards behind the ball, directly in line with my intended target, with the club in my right hand. As I let my senses absorb all the elements of the shot, I allow the club to swing gently back and forth, letting myself literally feel the coming shot. As I'm doing this, I let my imagination see the ball flying through the air to the target, its line and trajectory forming a visible path across the sky. I don't force the image to conform to what I want; if it doesn't come easily, that's a sign that I'm not ready to hit the shot, and I back away until the image does come easily. I've found that the clearer the picture, generally the better a shot I'll hit.

With a vivid image of my shot in my mind, and a corresponding feel in my hand, I stride to the ball, gripping the club with both hands and placing my right foot in its approximate address position. I'm still looking at the target, and I don't look down until I step forward with my left foot and assume my stance. Once I'm comfortable, I look at the target again, more intensely than ever. As I allow my senses to drink in the target, I rock gently from left foot to right foot in a rhythmic motion and simultaneously hold the clubhead slightly above the ball and waggle, letting my body really get the feel for the coming shot. I stop rocking when my body feels loose and ready to fire and my mind is locked into a by now very specific target. With that image in my mind's eye, I then make a swing that sends the ball to the target.

If at any point during my pre-shot routine I'm thinking of anything other than the target, I'm not being totally efficient. But if I've done things right, my only thought is where I want the ball to go.

It's amazing how often the ball does just that when you trust your target-oriented mind to direct your body in an instinctual, athletic way. I'll give you one example from the 1992 Masters. I had just bogeyed the twelfth hole and failed to birdie the thirteenth to fall two strokes behind Fred Couples, who was playing behind me. Then from the middle of the fairway on the fourteenth, with the pin in the back of the green over a huge knob, I mishit an 8-iron and left the ball in the one place you absolutely cannot leave it on that hole—short.

I knew I had "done the no," and the Masters was slipping away. When I got to my ball, I was faced with what legitimately could be called an impossible shot. The bank was only about 20 feet in front of me, and it rose 4 feet at a very steep angle, with the hole on a downslope only about 10 feet on the other side. If I had chosen to run the ball, it would have taken infinite touch to get it just to the top of the bank and let it trickle down to the hole.

In fact, even if I did it perfectly, it would still probably run by. And the risk was that I wouldn't get the ball to the top of the hill and I'd end up watching it roll past me back into the fairway.

There was no way to stop the ball by flying the bank. My only option if I wanted to give myself a realistic chance to save par was to punch the ball into the bank, hoping the upslope would kill it enough that it would take one bounce over the ledge and begin to bite.

Well, believe me, there was no way to consciously calculate this shot in terms of exactly where to land it or how hard to hit it. I just stared at it for a long time, letting my senses take in all the variables, literally letting my body feel the shot. I was totally trusting of whatever my body told me.

When I felt I had absorbed it, I took a 60-degree lob wedge and closed it down as far as possible. I wanted the most backspin on the lowest shot I could hit. It was the merging of two extremes. In my pre-shot, I looked at the bank, looked at the hole, and let the information filter to my hands. I didn't think of the potential disaster of landing too high up the bank, or even flying it completely, or chunking it short—all real possibilities. I thought only about what my mind's eye was seeing.

I hit the shot solid, and watched as the ball slammed into the bank, took one big hop nearly straight up in the air, just cleared the top of the ledge, took two quick bounces, and dived into the hole.

I have never made a more difficult shot from around the green, and certainly never in a bigger situation. It was probably the most amazing shot I've ever hit in my life. I didn't win the Masters, because Fred played great coming in, but that shot ranks as the greatest short-game shot of my career. It was eerie. It was the product of pure imagination, creativity, and all the resources that we have at our command but routinely underutilize. More than anything, it came from my intense focus on the target. That shot convinced me forever that there is no more powerful force in golf than the mind.

Visualization

In my experience, nothing ties the target to the swing like visualization. A player who learns how to unleash his imagination to create vivid images that his body responds to has found one of the most important keys to being a scorer.

Good players have always used visualization skills. Pros use the phrase "going to the movies" to describe imagining a shot before hitting it, and greats like Sam Snead and Jack Nicklaus made the process a part of every shot they hit. Visualization was a big part of my performance in golf and other sports long before I had ever heard the term.

The purpose of visualization is to create compelling mental images that make it easier for a person to do almost anything. Visualization techniques have been proven effective in all walks of life; they can work for short-term goals like hitting a good shot, or long-term goals like becoming the player you want to be. The power of the mind is so strong that if you can see yourself do it, you have a chance to do it.

Everyone visualizes differently. Some golfers can see clearly in real-life images; others get only vague pictures, while still others have the ability to create exaggerated images that make the task more vivid. The beauty of the process is that each person can choose the images that are most effective for him.

The possibilities are infinite. I've found that the more vivid I make my images, the more effective they are. I have imagined a tight fairway to be an inviting funnel that will take the ball to its center. When I'm putting, I might pretend the ball is a locomotive on tracks that go right into the hole; to make the image more intense, I've incorporated other senses by imagining the smell of smoke from the train's smokestack, or even hearing its whistle.

I don't mean to suggest that you can hit great shots only with a fertile, vivid imagination. Good psychology does not overcome bad physics, and no golfer can succeed without a grasp of physical fundamentals. But I believe a player can maximize his skills with good visualization skills.

If you have never tried to visualize, it might not come easily, but it's a skill that can be improved with practice. Spend some quiet time closing your eyes and letting your imagination create. Start by looking at an object, and then close your eyes and "see" it in your mind's eye. The better you get at reproducing a clear image, the better tools you'll have for strong visualization. Then start creating your own images. Remember, the more vivid and larger than life, the more effective they'll be.

The best I ever visualized was at the 1976 Masters. Without consciously making the effort, I was coming up to my ball and clearly seeing the flight I wanted for my next shot. I would see the flight of the ball all the way to its landing, and then kind of rewind it back into my mind. Then I would hit the shot; it was uncanny how often the ball would take the precise path I had seen. It was almost anticlimactic, as if I had already done it. I remember it was particularly effective on those 5-wood shots I hit to the par 5s, and I was 14 under on the par 5s for the week, a record. At that time, I had never heard anyone talking about visualization, and it was such an amazing thing that I almost felt like I was cheating.

Keeping out negative pictures

A fertile imagination is an asset if it's well directed, but the flip side is that it can also produce negative images. Just as a vivid positive image enhances performance, a powerful negative one can ruin it. In golf, you get what you think.

Negative thoughts come when you lose your connection with the target. It's fine to assess a shot and think, "I don't want to hit it there," but that's just a stop along the way to picking out the appropriate target. Once that target is chosen, you have to focus on where you want the ball to go, not where you don't want to hit it. When the "Don't hit it there!" thought or image intrudes after you've picked your target, a hesitant, fearful swing will result. And more often than not, because the brain responds to the strong negative image, the ball will end up right where you didn't want it to go.

Keeping negative images out takes willpower. You have to resolve to pick your target and think of nothing else.

This is easier to achieve when you're calm and free of distractions. Before playing, make a concerted effort to relax. Think of the positive images you'll be using on the course, so you get used to calling them up. Avoid rushing before the round. Resolve to stay composed and poised. Controlling your imagination comes from quieting your mind; then you can choose what you think.

Imagery and putting

Visualization and target orientation pay the biggest dividends in putting. I often get so caught up in my senses on the greens, it's as if I've literally "felt" the ball into the hole.

Of all the target-oriented images, I believe "seeing" a putt go into the hole is the easiest. Every time you assess a putt, you should see it toppling into the hole. If you don't, step away until you do. As you get ready to strike a putt, that image should have a relaxing, confidence-building effect. And if you trust that image and banish doubt and mechanical thoughts of how to stroke the putt, you will make more putts.

When visualizing a longer putt, let your eyes go over the entire line at the same speed the ball will travel. If you can make that image clear, your body will gain the right feel for the distance. Trust it.

Improving your swing through visualization

Visualization can help a scorer do more than hit shots at his target; strong images can also help him improve his golf swing.

Children often have wonderful golf swings because they're great at imitation. Adults tend to lose this ability as they get caught up in a world of explanation and analysis. Still, I think it's easier for most people to learn the correct movements in the swing by seeing someone do it than by having it explained. It's no accident that amateurs usually play better after having gone to a pro tournament or having watched one on television, because they then have a clearer picture of a good golf swing. It's the principle that made the "Sybervision" tapes of Al Geiberger and his wonderful swing so successful. I know I always seemed to swing better when I played with Sam Snead, because the image of his classic action got into my head.

You can make such an image a part of your arsenal by creating one: When you see an action that you admire—and one that's anatomically possible for you to aspire to—visualize it intensely so that it's burned in your memory. Then, when you're practicing, simply call it up and emulate it.

It's tempting to want to think of Tiger Woods or Fred Couples as models, but most of us can't swing as dynamically as those two. For normally built individuals, I think Hale Irwin and Annika Sorenstam provide wonderful models. Both of them have very sound setups, and each swings with simple ease and fluidity. Those are qualities we can all copy and learn from.

In a related way, you can build changes into your game with visualization techniques. Say you're working on keeping your right knee flexed on the backswing. Imagine the pin of a hand grenade attached to your pants that will be pulled out if your leg straightens. If you can make this image vivid and believable, chances are good you'll keep your right knee flexed.

Save swing thoughts for practice

Swing thoughts exist because we've all become so conditioned to working on our swing mechanics. There is nothing wrong with swing thoughts; they're among the most valuable tools a golfer has for getting better. But I believe that their place is on the practice tee, or during a casual round of swing experimentation—not during a competitive round of golf. That's when you want to play golf, not golf swing.

In my experience, trying to think your way through the golf swing during a round is a prescription for failure. The more you think about how you want to hit the ball, instead of where you want to hit it, the more difficult you're making the game. Swing thoughts take your mind off the target. They're a leading cause of golfers getting in their own way.

Swing thoughts create static. That vivid target image you visualized will be made fuzzy by thoughts like, "Get your left thumb under the shaft at the top," or "Rotate the left hip."

Swing thoughts will create less interference if you restrict them to the initial stage of your pre-shot routine. When you're behind the ball visualizing, a reminder about a change or adjustment you've been working on in practice can be helpful, but only if you can then put these conscious thoughts aside and let the target take over.

As far as actual thoughts during the swing go, the only ones I believe have any value other than those focused on the target have to do with feel or rhythm rather than mechanics or positions. Thinking about slowing down the swing, or making it smoother, or feeling the weight of the clubhead—these are ideas you can play with.

It's easy to get addicted to swing thoughts. If you've had success while playing with one before, you might feel you won't be able to play without one. It's human nature to want to "fix" the cause of a bad shot, and it's common on the PGA Tour to see players who've made a bad shot make a series of practice backswings looking back at the position of their hands. This is courting trouble.

The hurdle that players who rely on swing thoughts have to get over is trust. If you've got good fundamentals, you already know how to make a good swing. All you need then is a mental commitment to the target and the trust that your body will respond. You can't do that if you're trying to think your way through the golf swing.

I know, because I haven't always practiced what I'm preaching. As much as I've known the pitfalls, I've fallen back on swing thoughts many times. The biggest reason was the swing change I made in mid-career to keep from laying the club off at the top of my backswing. As many balls as I hit on the practice range, it was a very difficult change to ingrain; for several years, I didn't trust that I could perform the correct move without consciously thinking about it. I found a way to play fairly effectively with one swing thought, but I almost never played well if I had two. Forget three.

The only time I ever won with two swing thoughts was at Doral in 1981, and that was probably the most stressful four rounds I've ever played because I felt like the only thing keeping me from hitting a poor shot was the very difficult task of keeping my thoughts straight while I swung. It's funny, though, because even then, in the latter stages of the fourth round I found a rhythm and started playing more on feel and my instinct for the target. I came to the seventy-second with a one-stroke lead over David Graham. As you may know, the 437-yard eighteenth at Doral is one of the hardest driving holes in golf (even before I redesigned it in 1997 to make it tougher). A very narrow fairway is bordered by water all the way down the left side, with thick banyan trees on the right. That day, a strong wind was blowing in from the left, making the hole play its most difficult. You would think my swing-thought fetish would really kick in, yet when I walked on the tee, I suddenly "saw" a beautiful drive that headed down the middle before drawing perfectly to an inlet of fairway over the right corner of the lake. I was visualizing big-time, and wouldn't you know it, that was exactly the drive I hit. That drive helped me get out of the swing-thought habit.

The fact is, when I've played my best rounds, I've had exactly zero swing thoughts. And in the last decade or so, I've almost totally abandoned them. In retrospect, if I had taken that approach in the '60s, '70s, and early '80s, I think I would have won more tournaments.

Abandon yours. The next round you play, make a conscious effort to eliminate any swing thoughts, and replace them with an intense concentration on the target. If you hit some bad shots, adjust by increasing your focus on the target, not by trying to adjust your swing. You will play better.

See your next round

A very effective way to improve is to visualize an entire round before playing it. Scorers, particularly before competitive rounds, do this all the time.

What's valuable about playing a course in your head is the sense of orderliness it can bring to your play. By seeing yourself hitting the proper shot hole after hole, you'll develop a strategic plan that will reduce poor decisions and wasted strokes. Just knowing what would constitute a perfect round, even if you can't live up to it, will give you an improved blueprint to follow.

Another advantage an imaginary round can provide is to reduce the fear factor. Most golf courses have some scary holes, and playing them in your head can prepare you emotionally. Visualize yourself being relaxed and with full concentration on the target as you step up to a difficult shot you're likely to face; when the real situation arises, it will be easier for you to avoid the pitfalls that fear and negative images can induce.

The key is to create an image of yourself approaching situations with a sound strategy and a strong mental process; seeing yourself hitting wonderful shots certainly won't hurt, either. For professionals, such an approach is an important part of pretournament preparation. Make it part of your routine as well.

Memory banking

Another form of visualization is what I call *memory banking*. When you hit a great shot, really absorb its path and the sensation of hitting it and watching it, and file it away so you can call on it as a positive image in the future.

This is what I did with that 50-foot birdie putt I made at

Shinnecock that turned the championship around for me. I've seen videotapes of the putt, and my reaction seemed almost calculated: Instead of celebrating after the putt went in, I just stared at the hole for several seconds, as if "recording" the trail of that putt in my mind. I locked it away, and believe me, I've drawn on that putt many times since then.

As you fill your memory bank, it won't be long before you have a file of wonderful images you can call on for every club in the bag.

Take five

A great exercise for developing target awareness and visualization is to play a few holes with only a 5-iron. Because you'll almost never have a regular 5-iron shot, you'll have to improvise continually. You'll find that hitting a 5-iron 75 yards or so requires extra concentration on the target in order to get the right feel for the distance, and having to manuever running shots around bunkers and humps will make you use visualization skills. When you go back to playing with a full set, your mental game and your ability to improvise will be sharper.

The zone

"The zone" is a performance state where things seem to move in slow motion, potential distractions don't register, and the task seems easy. Nothing bothers you, you're walking light, your swing seems automatic, and the hole looks big.

When I've been in the zone, it's usually for only a few holes at a time. On rare occasions, it lasts a whole round. On only two occasions in my career have I sustained that state for essentially the whole tournament: in the 1976 Masters, when I shot the 271 that tied Jack Nicklaus for the record that stood until Tiger Woods broke it in 1997, and to a slightly lesser extent in the 1982 PGA at Southern Hills, where I opened with 63 and stayed in command throughout to win easily.

When I'm in the zone, I get that glassy-eyed, penetrating stare that Maria named "The Look" after I won at Shinnecock. "I've seen him win without that look," she told the press, "but I've never seen him lose with it." When I've had it, it's given me a presence that projects total confidence and concentration. Some players have said it makes me an intimidating player, but believe me, I'm never trying to scare anybody out there. "The Look" is simply my expression when I'm using my mind effectively. It's a state where the club feels wonderful in my hands, and my only thoughts are on the shot at hand.

Looking back at the occasions when I've been in the zone, I can see something of a pattern. I got in the zone more frequently during those periods when I was immersed in the game, single-minded about my goal of being the best I could be, prepared mentally and physically, and truly enjoyed the challenge. In that state, I could best see the beauty of the game and how it should be played. As we're constantly discovering, what the mind can see, it can do.

The zone is elusive. As much as I've tried, I've never been able to visualize quite like I did that week at Augusta. You tend to fall out of the zone as soon as you start thinking you might be in it. In golf, trying to "make" things happen usually just makes the game more difficult.

I'm convinced, however, that the secret of the zone lies in total commitment to the target—shot after shot after shot. Finding out how to get in the zone more often is the next frontier in golf.

C h a p t e r   1 0

Attitude

Golf has got to be the most elusive game. As much as we seek consistency, its only constant is constant change. Driving accuracy, swing tempo, concentration, putting confidence, you name it—there's really no guarantee any one of them will be in top shape when you need it.

I'm going to propose one exception to the rule, however, as a part of your arsenal that is repeatable, reliable, and—once you fully understand its value—should never leave you.

Attitude.

In my opinion, "attitude" is the most underrated word in golf. A good one is essential to enjoyment, to improvement, and, of course, to being a scorer. It takes time, but once you fully grasp and appreciate how valuable a good attitude is, the incentive to keep it is considerable.

Naturally, that appreciation doesn't come easily. Golf, when you're trying to play it as well as you can, is a series of unfulfilled hopes. Without the protective armor of a good attitude, the disappointments can undermine your performance and leave you with some wounds that won't heal.

A scorer learns to understand and overcome the powerful internal forces that can regularly ruin a round. Some golfers are fortunate enough to sense the value of a good attitude at a young age; they develop perspective, maturity, and toughness well beyond their years. For most of us, a good attitude comes with experience, usually after learning the hard way that raging against the difficulty and unfairness of the game is useless. For too many others, a good attitude never comes at all.

It's very easy to have a bad attitude toward golf. There are so many things that can go wrong, so many times when the game is cruel. It's an endless cycle of negativity if you let it be.

I could name many highly talented players who should have made more of their ability but lacked a good attitude; I cannot think of one enduring champion who had a poor one. The greatest of them all, Jack Nicklaus, has always had a model attitude. Nobody competed harder, but no one lost more graciously. When I think of Jack trying to win a tournament, I think of a man with an inner peace that made him unafraid to lose.

I learned from these and other positive players, and I think that for the latter half of my career in particular, I've had a very good attitude. As a young man, I hadn't fully understood its importance; like a lot of talented but undisciplined players, I was on the arrogant side. I complained about bad breaks, battled my temper, and looked for excuses when things didn't go right.

My attitude improved dramatically when I finally realized— after nearly a decade of underachieving as a professional and being beaten down by the game's disappointments—that if I truly wanted to be as good as I could be, a good attitude would be as essential as a good swing or putting stroke. In fact, it would be the catalyst that improved every part of my game.

A renewed attitude was a vital part of my prime years in the mid-1970s and 1980s, and was the most important factor in keeping me competitive in major championships into the 1990s. Today, I believe I play golf for the right reasons. Certainly I play to win, because it's my profession. But I also play because it has enhanced friendships, brought me closer to my two sons, and taught me about life. People with good attitudes are winners. They know how to turn negatives into positives. Most of all, they know how to enjoy the ride.

Nothing will get you through the mental mine fields the game puts before you better than a good attitude. Let it be your most reliable weapon.

Enjoy the walk

First and foremost, a good attitude lets you have fun playing golf.

It's easy to forget that fun is the most basic reason we play. Whether it's the distance the ball travels through the air, or the way golf builds character, my enjoyment of golf has always been enhanced when I've taken a step back and simply appreciated how much the game offers.

Looking back, I can see how Arnold Palmer had a tremendous influence on me in this area, although it took me a while to figure it out. Arnold was my golfing idol growing up, and when I joined the tour in 1963, he was in his prime. He was wonderful to me, inviting me to play practice rounds and allowing me to pick his brain. But it was Arnold's outlook and the way he behaved that left an impression on me that grew and became more important as I got older.

Very simply, Arnold loved, and loves, what he's doing, and no matter how worn he was from the demands of his popularity or disappointed by a bad round, he always carried and projected himself as a very lucky person. It couldn't have been an act; it was something Arnold believed. I've learned to believe it about myself as well, and Arnold's example helped me build a perspective and inner stability that's been invaluable to my golf career.

It's easy to enjoy golf when you're playing well, but you really need the deeper perspective a good attitude gives you if you're playing badly. When I'm disappointed or mad at the way I'm playing, if I've just missed a short putt or hit one out of bounds or blown a tournament, I've trained myself to remember that there is nothing else in the world I'd rather be doing; I'm in beautiful surroundings, playing the game I love, with people who are my friends, and I'm being paid for it. I couldn't be luckier. When I feel negativity coming on, I always tell myself, "Enjoy your walk."

Now that might sound artificial, and to be honest, when you're grinding hard trying to win a tournament and you make a mistake, comparing the very intense undertaking you're engaged in to a walk in the park is mostly a mental device. It helps make bad results tolerable, so you can put them behind you and get back in the present where you need to be. But it works, and the reason it works is that, on a profound level, it's the truth. In golf and in life, it's ultimately the journey, not the destination, that must bring you satisfaction. Enjoy the walk golf provides.

Be patient

A scorer knows that while golf constantly tempts us with shots that offer a chance for instant gratification, the game over the long haul is best played within one's capabilities. That takes patience.

"Patience" is the word you hear constantly when pros analyze their performances, particularly in major championships. In that context, patience means adhering to a game plan of conservative, steady play even when it doesn't seem to be paying off.

But patience also means knowing that your practice and hard work will pay off, and understanding that improvement often comes in plateaus rather than at a steady rate.

Finally, a scorer is patient because he has faith in himself and in his approach. A golfer who believes in himself doesn't panic or lose his composure when things go wrong. He calmly rights the ship, bears down, and waits for things to go his way. Jack Nicklaus has often been admired for his patience on the golf course, and it's no coincidence that no player I've ever seen has believed in himself more than Jack.

This kind of confidence doesn't just happen. But to develop patience, it's important to have a plan for yourself that you believe in—whether it's for the way you want to swing or the strategy you want to employ. If you're truly committed to your plan, you won't abandon it so easily when things go badly—especially if you accept that there will be shots and holes and rounds when things go badly. When you believe in your plan and believe in your ability to carry it out, patience is your ally.

Respect yourself

I've said it before, but it bears repeating: Golf is hard.

Respecting the challenge of the game is vital to having a good attitude. Appreciating how difficult golf is makes good rounds that much more satisfying, and bad ones less an occasion for despair than an opportunity for learning.

Just as vital is respecting yourself. I know that can be especially difficult for less accomplished players; the game gives you so much time and opportunity to beat yourself up. But if you don't like who you are on the golf course, or if you fail to give yourself credit for taking on the game's challenge, you'll never learn the crucial skill of forgiving yourself when you don't succeed. Self-loathing, at every level of ability, will eventually keep you from getting better.

Even if it seems artificial, force yourself to be positive. A scorer has a healthy ego, because he realizes that just by enduring the obstacles golf throws at him and still striving to get better, he's doing something that will make him a stronger person. I know my character has been improved by what the game has taught me, and it makes me proud to be a golfer, no matter how badly I might play. And when I play well, I feel worthy of the rewards.

I lapse, of course. My attitude flags when I'm tired, when I'm frustrated with my game, when there is too much on my mind. I have to fight becoming like too many other golfers we all know who are constantly complaining—about their swings, their clubs, the golf course, their playing partners ad nauseam. One way I stop myself from complaining is by realizing that such behavior shows a lack of inner belief and a lack of self-respect. The complainer is preparing to lose by building up excuses in advance. I don't want to be that kind of golfer, and you shouldn't either.

Anger

Having a good attitude means being able to manage anger. It doesn't mean never getting angry; I've never met a golfer who was any good who didn't get hot. If you care, if you want to win, if you have high standards, you are going to feel that burning psychological and physiological reaction that is anger when things go wrong.

The key is not to let it negatively affect your performance. It's not an easy task. The problem of managing anger is probably the main reason most golfers don't reach their primes until their thirties. It often takes that long to find the way to either channel or to get rid of anger. Some players never do.

When you give in to anger, it makes you rush. It clouds your judgment. It makes you physically tense, causes poor rhythm and other swing flaws, and especially impairs your ability to pull off delicate shots. You start making more mistakes and don't stop until the anger is finally gone. Inevitably, you "lose it."

The most fundamentally damaging thing anger does is to cause you to look backward instead of being in the present. When you're angry it's because of something that's already happened; this means you're not focusing on the task at hand, which is the first rule of being a scorer.

A scorer has to realize that anger is doing him no good, and it must be gone before he hits his next shot. That takes discipline. Some players have novel ways of getting rid of anger. Greg Norman secretly pinches himself very hard just below the ribs. Tom Watson, when he hits a bad shot, forces himself to watch it until it comes to a dead stop. "My punishment," he calls it. Other players may rage at a caddy who has been warned that it will be part of his job to absorb unwarranted abuse on such occasions. (I don't advise your trying this at your club, unless you do it where no one else can hear you—and you tip very, very well.)

I don't do anything very elaborate. My temper was never the explosive kind even when I was young, and as I got older I got better at making sure anger didn't eat at me. Knowing that it could ruin my concentration, distract my playing partners, and cause me to make a fool of myself, I saw there was no upside to staying real mad. So when the anger rose and breaking a club seemed tempting, I just learned to swallow hard and let the moment pass. It's a conscious decision, and it's hard to do at first—but like anything else, the more you do it, the better you get at it.

Eventually, it can become a source of pride. I want to consider myself, and be considered, mentally tough, and losing your temper is mentally weak. Once I decided that having a good attitude was part of being a winner, I associated letting anger get the best of me with being a loser. In the final analysis, losing your temper is quitting, and if you truly want to be a scorer, you don't quit.

Pressure

A more complicated force than anger is pressure. The first thing I want to say about pressure in golf is that it's powerful; it may be self-induced, but that doesn't mean a player can just make it go away. It's inevitable that the more you want to do well, the more you want to win and the more expectations you have, the more pressure you'll feel. The challenge comes in developing an attitude that understands, accepts, and finally even welcomes pressure.

Pressure comes from fear. It can be the fear of being embarrassed by a poor performance in front of friends and peers, which is a common fear among social golfers. Among players who play competitive golf, pressure comes from fear of losing. The closer you come to winning, the more losing hurts. When you lose close ones, you open up psychic wounds that you'll carry the rest of your life, no matter how deeply you succeed in burying them. I think the reason a lot of players aren't winners is because coming close and losing is just too painful; to protect themselves, they avoid coming close.

We admire champions for their skill, but most of all for the way they perform at their best when the pressure is greatest. It's a great quality, deserving of our respect, but it doesn't have to be rare. Pressure is suffocating if you let it be, but you can also learn to use its power to help you perform better. The key lies in a good attitude.

During my career on the regular tour, I gained a reputation for being a good pressure player. If I was, I believe it was mainly because of my attitude. First, I acknowledge pressure. Because I care very much about how I perform and my record as a golfer, pressure is a given for me. It's an obstacle, and I have to deal with it if I want to be successful.

The first lessons I received on how to stay positive and strong under pressure came while I was playing for my own money as a teenager in fairly high-stakes gambling games. I found out early in those $10 and $20 nassaus that if I lost my poise or my temper, or felt sorry for myself, it was only going to cause me to dig into my pocket for money I couldn't really afford to lose. I learned in the most direct way possible that becoming negative doesn't help you win, and I liked to win too much to let myself self-destruct. I also learned from gambling that you don't give your opponent an edge by showing your emotions or disappointment, and I think that outward control helped me stay even and poised on the inside as well. Something was telling me that I would have to know how to handle pressure if I made golf my career, so I sought out situations to test myself.

As a professional golfer who wanted to win tournaments and major championships, I had to be able to enjoy being in position to win them. If I felt otherwise, my chances of winning were greatly reduced and probably destroyed. I knew it would hurt tremendously if I lost, particularly if I threw a tournament away. But as a competitor, I couldn't give in to that fear.

What I finally evolved into was a sense of peace. Because I'm doing what I love to do, and giving it my best effort, I can take whatever consequences come with it. I don't have to be afraid of a bitter defeat because I've already accepted in advance that it's part of the entire experience of competition. Bottom line, I know I have an attitude that can take the heat.

It's been tested, believe me. I was devastated when I lost the 1990 Masters. I led nearly the entire tournament, was four strokes ahead with nine holes to go, but ended up losing in sudden death to Nick Faldo.

That memory hurts, and always will. Not only would I have become the oldest winner of the tournament at age forty-seven, I would have been the first winner who also won the ceremonial par-3 tournament in the same year. The Masters has always been my favorite event, and it would have been my second green jacket.

Many people thought I would never recover. I wasn't sure myself. It's funny, though—I did, and it took only a few days before I arose from bed and saw it all clearly. I had competed as hard as I could, made two crucial mistakes, and got beaten. I had put myself where I wanted to be my whole career, in a position from which I had won many times before—but this time, the pressure got me. It was painful, but I realized I still loved what I did for a living, still considered it a great challenge, and still had a great desire to be in the same position again. Very simply, just as I had accepted winning four other major championships, I had to accept losing this one. If I was a player with the right attitude, as I believed I was, I would handle this and not be afraid the next time I was under pressure.

I found out I could take the heat. In 1992, I won at Doral at age forty-nine, allowing me to set a record for the span between first and last victories on the PGA Tour. The very next month, I nearly won the Masters again, finishing second to Fred Couples. In 1993, at the age of fifty-one, I was chosen to play in my eighth Ryder Cup, becoming the oldest competitor in the event's history. I was the leading point producer on the American team, and on the very tense final day of singles, I won the cup's clinching point when I defeated José-María Olazabal 2 up in one of the most pressure-packed situations I've ever known.

My match with José was the third match from the last. After leaving the eleventh green all even, I checked the scoreboard and saw that U.S. players were losing in most of the matches ahead of me, meaning our team was in real danger of losing the Ryder Cup. At the twelfth hole, I hit a 2-iron to 4 feet and won the hole; I birdied the thirteenth; and on the fifteenth I hit the flag with my approach. It was one of the best stretches of clutch golf I've ever played, and I owed it to my attitude.

Of course, I still sometimes fail under pressure. At the 1998 Senior Open at Riviera, I was leading by three strokes after 54 holes, and playing very solidly. But on Sunday, under pressure, my game just wasn't there. I shot a 73 that allowed Hale Irwin to pass me, and I finished third. Had I won, I would have become the only player to win all four of the senior major championships, an accomplishment I would have been very proud of. But I was also proud of the way I had battled for 72 holes. My performance at Riviera told me that, at age fifty-six, I can still win championships. And if I get in contention again, I'll still welcome both the pressure and the opportunity.

Playing well under pressure is a learning process. The first time you face what feels like overwhelming pressure, whether it comes in your first tournament, the first time you play for $5, or just hitting in front of a lot of people on a crowded first tee, you'll probably fail. You'll be unable to think clearly, you'll rush—even feel some panic—and you'll almost certainly hit a bad shot.

I remember walking to the first tee of my first Ryder Cup in 1969 and being barely able to breathe. My partner was Miller Barber; we were the first group off in the alternate-shot format, and since we had the honor, we were hitting the very first shots of the matches. We had decided the night before that Miller would hit on the odd-numbered holes, which meant he would drive off No. 1. Well, when we got to the tee, "X," as we all call Miller, kind of stood there, and without looking at me said in that real fast way of his, "You hit it, Junior." He was scared to death, and he wasn't ashamed to admit it. Well, I almost fainted, but I managed to get the ball airborne. Miller and I, a couple of nervous cats, lost that match 3 and 2 to Neil Coles and Brian Huggett. It was the pressure.

THE ELEMENTS OF SCORING

Don't be ashamed when pressure gets the best of you. Acknowledge it, and figure out what the forces were that beat you; if you don't, you'll always be weak under pressure. I find athletes and golfers who try to deny that pressure exists are generally the ones affected by it most. If you're going to be a scorer, understand that every time you play under pressure is a golden opportunity to get better. As Michael Jordan says in his commercial, "I fail constantly. And that is why I succeed." Think of it as a thrill ride—the scary part makes it fun. That's what Jack Nicklaus calls it. I remember Jack's response after he won the 1975 Masters in that great duel with Tom Weiskopf and Johnny Miller: "It was fun," he said. "You're inspired, you're eager, you're excited . . . I've never had more fun in my life."

Now, none of us is Jack Nicklaus, but the feelings he described are the result of turning pressure into a source of positive, rather than negative, energy. Sure you're nervous, but if you let yourself relish the challenge, you can channel that energy into a mental focus that can actually bring out your very best golf. Have you ever noticed how many sudden-death playoffs on the PGA Tour end with someone holing a long putt? It's the result of nervous but positive-thinking players turning heightened senses into heightened performance.

To get more familiar with pressure, I recommend playing gambling games on the course and on the practice green. Not for anything exorbitant, but enough so it hurts to lose. I don't call it gambling, anyway; I call it practicing winning.

And when you play or practice alone, you can simulate pressure. On the putting green, try to make ten 3-footers in a row (going back to zero if you miss), and notice how your throat tightens and your hands get clammy after you make eight. Or engage in that solitary exercise every good golfer I've ever known has acted out—pretending to be in contention down the stretch of a major championship, playing against Hogan, or Palmer, or

Nicklaus, or Woods, or whoever, and making each shot crucial. It may sound silly, but your imagination can induce a lot of nervousness. Get to recognize and understand those feelings, and you're on your way to learning how to handle pressure.

Remember: No one is pressure-proof. The best players have accepted that there are times when you handle it and times when you don't. The important thing is that you not run away from it.

Confidence under pressure is earned. As long as you keep your attitude strong and pay attention to your reactions, the more you're under pressure, the more you'll progress as a player.

Responsibility

Some people believe that a golfer should always find something other than himself—a caddy, clubs, the course architect—to blame for a bad shot or performance, so that his confidence won't be eroded.

Not me. I believe that a golfer will develop a much stronger attitude and be a much better player if he accepts the idea that everything that happens to him on the golf course is his responsibility.

My reason is simple: Blaming an outside force may feel good in the short term, but excuses keep a player from developing the mental strength needed to deal with adversity. When you come to believe that nothing is your fault, it gives you an unconscious "out" for giving in to pressure or difficulty or anger. To my way of thinking, that can only undermine your confidence.

When you take responsibility for your mistakes and predicaments, you learn to accept that golf is a tough game at which you're often going to come up short. This truth alone is relaxing, because it makes inevitable failures more understandable. It also reminds you that you're resilient, which should increase your confidence.

To me, Tom Watson has always been a model of the responsible player. After a bad shot, Watson never shows any outward signs of being down or negative. He accepts the consequences and then does everything in his power to hit the very best shot possible from the predicament he's in. I've never seen one player follow a poor shot with a great shot so often. Tom seems to relish the challenge of recovering from a bad shot. This attitude always puts him in that most important of all golfing states—the present.

Tom has never been afraid of admitting mistakes, and he talked openly about his problem with short putts over the last several years. It was as if Tom was challenging himself to conquer a problem that to many pros is so terrifying it's unspeakable. Watson's mental toughness is such that he overcame the yips and won two tournaments at the age of forty-eight.

Acknowledging and seeking to understand the cause of mistakes is part of being a scorer. The week before the 1986 U.S. Open, I had held the lead going into the final round at Westchester only to blow up with a 77. I was in no mood to rehash that collapse, but on the 100-mile drive to Shinnecock Hills, Maria insisted I confront what had happened. I resisted because I just wanted to forget that it ever happened at all, but we finally talked out how I had lost my focus in the final round. I'm convinced that talk and the awareness it produced helped me play the most focused round of my life during the last day at Shinnecock.

A more recent example occurred at the 1994 PGA Seniors. I held a three-stroke lead on the fifteenth in the final round when I pushed three balls into the water and made an 8. It hurt, but I admitted publicly that I had allowed pressure to cause me to revert to some old swing habits. The short-term pain of talking about it helped get rid of some long-term hurt, and at the same time increased my resolve to make sure the same thing never happened again. At the same tournament the next year, I carried myself with extra determination and won by five strokes.

Don't take the easy way out and make excuses. Take responsibility, and you will be a better player.

Believe what you have to believe

Another form of mental strength is the ability to believe. In order to boost his confidence, a scorer will convince himself of things that will help him perform. Although they might not be things he would think if the only critieria were truth or logic, tweaking his opinion makes perfect sense when it comes to scoring.

For example, a scorer might not like a particular golf course, but if he's playing it in competition, he finds a way to tell himself it suits his strengths. He might not generally like talking a lot on the golf course, but when he's paired with an extroverted partner he tells himself that conversing while playing relaxes him. Although he may prefer fast greens, he doesn't tell himself that when he putts on slow ones. When he's facing a tee shot that resulted in a snap-hook out of bounds the last time he played it, he finds a way to completely expunge that shot from his memory.

Gary Player is the absolute best at these mental gymnastics. Some of his peers may think Gary is being insincere, but at the moment that he's expressing his flexible views, he really believes them. His purpose is simply to give himself the greatest chance to perform his best. Conversely, if Lee Trevino had been able to convince himself that he liked Augusta National, I'm sure he would have contended in many Masters, and probably at some point won the tournament.

In golf, you get what you think, and a scorer becomes very adept at controlling what he thinks. He knows that when it comes to his thoughts, he has a choice.

Putting is attitude

I am a good putter. I know it and I believe it. If I didn't believe it, I wouldn't be a good putter.

Every scorer should feel this way. Although putting certainly requires some talent, the mechanical demands are minimal. I honestly believe that with a strong mind, you can literally will the ball into the hole.

I have a nonperfectionist attitude toward putting. By that I mean I don't think that only a perfect putt will go in. The hole is $4\frac{1}{4}$ inches wide, which allows a putt hit at good speed almost 2 inches on either side of the ideal line to fall in. I remind myself of this margin for error to avoid the trap of thinking that a putt has to be flawlessly read and struck; that kind of attitude creates tension, and makes putting very frustrating. I suggest you take the more fatalistic view that great putters like Dave Stockton and Ben Crenshaw (and I) take: Believe with all your heart you are going to make the putt, hit the best putt you can, and whatever happens, remember you're a good putter. Don't ever forget it.

Get rid of expectations

Expectations are very dangerous things in golf. Especially when you've worked hard to improve, it's natural to expect some reward. But there are no guarantees in golf, and having expectations only creates pressure and increases the chance for disappointment.

Rather than expectations, I prefer to have hopes. Although I'm confident of my ability to succeed, I play my best when I hope for the best but am prepared for the worst. When I tee off, I expect only two things of myself—to enjoy my walk, and to give my all on every shot. I've found this to be the most useful attitude.

Let your attitude get better with age

Attitude is the one place an older golfer has an advantage. Especially by age fifty, a scorer has perspective and wisdom that should give him a formidable mental game.

It's certainly been true in my own case. The best proof came after our home in Miami, which our family had lived in for nearly twenty years, burned down in February of 1992. The aftermath of that fire is the hardest thing I've ever gone through, and I was devastated; so was Maria, but she snapped back faster than I did. The Doral Ryder Open was coming up, and I was considering withdrawing until Maria, in typical fashion, told me, "I'll take care of everything with the house. You just go play golf. This family needs something positive to happen."

Her attitude inspired me to do my part. I resolved to channel everything I was feeling into playing the best golf I could. All during the week of the Doral, there didn't seem to be anything the game could throw at me that could divert me from my task. The fire had taught me again, and more than ever, that golf was a game, but also one that you could play with every fiber of your being. I've never played with such a combination of peace and purpose, and I won the tournament by two strokes, becoming at forty-nine the oldest winner of a regular tour event since Art Wall in 1975. That week, I put all the lessons to work.

Our ability to appreciate is enhanced as we get older, and appreciation itself is a performance enhancer. Remember that you are playing a marvelous game that you can play for a lifetime. Enjoy it, and be thankful. With that attitude, you win every day.